T0334070

Cambridge Elements ☰

Elements in Pragmatics
edited by
Jonathan Culpeper
Lancaster University, UK
Michael Haugh
University of Queensland, Australia

PRAGMATIC INFERENCE

Misunderstandings, Accountability, Deniability

Chi-Hé Elder
University of East Anglia

CAMBRIDGE
UNIVERSITY PRESS

Shaftesbury Road, Cambridge CB2 8EA, United Kingdom

One Liberty Plaza, 20th Floor, New York, NY 10006, USA

477 Williamstown Road, Port Melbourne, VIC 3207, Australia

314–321, 3rd Floor, Plot 3, Splendor Forum, Jasola District Centre,
New Delhi – 110025, India

103 Penang Road, #05–06/07, Visioncrest Commercial, Singapore 238467

Cambridge University Press is part of Cambridge University Press & Assessment,
a department of the University of Cambridge.

We share the University's mission to contribute to society through the pursuit of
education, learning and research at the highest international levels of excellence.

www.cambridge.org
Information on this title: www.cambridge.org/9781009500838

DOI: 10.1017/9781009036672

First published 2024

A catalogue record for this publication is available from the British Library.

ISBN 978-1-009-50083-8 Hardback
ISBN 978-1-009-00570-8 Paperback
ISSN 2633-6464 (online)
ISSN 2633-6456 (print)

Pragmatic Inference

Misunderstandings, Accountability, Deniability

Elements in Pragmatics

DOI: 10.1017/9781009036672
First published online: February 2024

Chi-Hé Elder
University of East Anglia
Author for correspondence: Chi-Hé Elder, c.elder@uea.ac.uk

Abstract: The concept of inference is foundational to the study of pragmatics; however, the way it is theoretically conceptualised and methodologically operationalised is far from uniform. This Element investigates the role that inference plays in pragmatic models of communication, bringing together a range of scholarship that characterises inference in different ways for different purposes. It addresses the nature of 'faulty inferences', promoting the study of misunderstandings as crucial for understanding inferential processes, and looks at sociopragmatic issues such as the role of commitment, accountability, and deniability of inferences in interpersonal communication. This Element highlights that the question of where the locus of meaning lies is not only relevant to pragmatic theory but is also of paramount importance for understanding and managing real-life interpersonal communication conflict.

Keywords: pragmatic inference, commitment, misunderstanding, accountability, deniability

ISBNs: 9781009500838 (HB), 9781009005708 (PB), 9781009036672 (OC)
ISSNs: 2633-6464 (online), 2633-6456 (print)

Contents

1 Pragmatic Inference: A Concept with Many Faces

Inference, broadly speaking, is the deriving of conclusions from facts or evidence. Inference can be thought of as either the conclusion itself, or the process of deriving that conclusion. Inferential processes can take different forms – such as deductive, inductive, or abductive – and different kinds of processes can take different kinds of information as their inputs.

This Element is about a specific kind of inference, namely *pragmatic inference.* Pragmatic inference is a heterogeneous concept, but, roughly speaking, it is the deriving of conclusions about meaning based on linguistic communication. From now on, if we drop the prefix 'pragmatic' in favour of simply referring to 'inferences' and 'inferential processes', bear in mind that these are in reference to the study of language and meaning, unless otherwise specified.

A prudent first question to ask is: why study pragmatic inference in the first place? Well, until the 1970s, it wasn't widely studied in linguistics. It was assumed that if speakers communicate their messages directly and explicitly, hearers – assuming they 'speak the same language' – should have no problem understanding what the speaker said, as all they have to do is 'decode' the message using their knowledge of the linguistic system of the language they speak. But the problem is that speakers do not always – or arguably ever – convey messages directly and explicitly. In fact, it wouldn't be efficient to try: the physical (vocal or gestural) apparatus that speakers have for conveying thoughts is grossly limited in scope compared to the richness of human cognition, creating a bottleneck in communication; as Levinson (2000: 29) says, 'inference is cheap, articulation is expensive'. So while meanings can be conveyed more or less directly via the language system of whatever natural language (English, French, Japanese, etc.) they use, speakers can communicate much more information than that encoded by the words uttered, which hearers can then infer. This Element discusses various ways in which scholars have studied pragmatic inference, as well as various issues that have arisen alongside those studies.

1.1 Some Ways to Study Pragmatic Inference

The study of pragmatic inference came to the fore in Anglo-American pragmatic theory through Grice's (1975, 1978) work on conversational implicatures: aspects of meaning that go beyond the explicit content of 'what is said'. This work put focus on the role of speakers' intentions in the recovery of meaning, challenging the traditional 'code model' that assumed language to 'encode' meanings to be 'decoded' by hearers. Rather, Grice's theory of speaker meaning proposed that successful communication relies on speakers abiding by the Cooperative Principle, 'Make your conversational contribution such as is required, at the stage at which it occurs, by the accepted purpose or direction of the talk exchange in which you are engaged' (Grice 1989: 26), and the four categories of conversational maxims, of quantity ('make your contribution as informative as required' but 'do not make your contribution more informative than is required'), quality ('try to make your contribution one that is true'), relation ('be relevant') and manner ('be perspicuous'). In case a speaker intends to communicate a conversational implicature, that is, something other than what was explicitly said, a hearer is licensed to infer that implicitly communicated meaning on the assumption that the speaker is a rational communicator who is following the Cooperative Principle and the maxims (see Grice 1975, 'Logic and Conversation' for his classic examples).

Implicatures are typically viewed as the archetype of pragmatic inference, and differ in important ways from *logical inference*, that is, conclusions derived from premises via valid arguments. This is not to say that logical inference does not also play an important role in the study of language and meaning: if I know some sentence to be true, I can construct inferences about the world based on the facts described by that sentence. For example, if I know that all sheep are mammals, and I know that Dolly is a sheep, then I can infer – via deductive inference – that Dolly is a mammal. But logical inference differs from pragmatic inference insofar as it is typically monotonic: the conclusion cannot be changed with the addition of new premises. Pragmatic inference, by contrast, is usually *non-monotonic*. This is because when hearers make inferences about what speakers say, they do so on the basis of partial evidence, and the conclusions they draw can be overridden (or 'cancelled') in the face of new, competing, information (see Section 4 on cancellation). In other words, pragmatic inferences are *defeasible*. This was, in fact, one of Grice's tests for an aspect of meaning constituting an implicature, as opposed to, say, an entailment (a fact that logically follows from what is said): implicatures are defeasible, while entailments are not, and presuppositions (background information that is required for comprehending what has been said) lie somewhere in the middle (see Beaver et al. 2021 on presuppositional inferences).

Assuming that 'speakers implicate, hearers infer' (Horn 2004: 6), pragmatic inference is very often equated with the hearer's recovery of the speaker's intended meaning. One direction in which scholars have since reframed Grice's original philosophical account of speaker meaning is to address the question: *how* do hearers infer what speakers mean from what they say? One of the most notable developments in this regard is due to Relevance Theory (Sperber and Wilson 1986/1995), that aims to explain the cognitive processes in which a hearer engages in order to recover a speaker's intended meaning. This explanation relies on the notion of 'relevance'. An assumption is relevant in a context if it yields high cognitive effects (changes to one's immediate and manifest cognitive environment) alongside low processing effort. The crux of their theory of language processing is that pragmatic *inferencing* can be reduced to two principles of relevance: first, 'human cognition tends to be geared to the maximisation of relevance', and second, 'every act of ostensive communication communicates a presumption of its own optimal relevance' (Sperber and Wilson 1986/1995: 260). If a hearer presumes a speaker to be abiding by these principles, hearers recover speakers' intended meanings through a process of least effort: a trade-off between maximising cognitive effects and minimising processing effort. This is a subtle move in focus away from offering generalisations of speakers' language use in the spirit of Grice, and towards a psychological account of utterance processing that addresses the cognitive question of how hearers recover speakers' intentions.

In addition to the questions of *what* pragmatic inference is, as well as the question of *how* pragmatic inference is derived in the mind, there is also the question of *why*, under particular circumstances, would a hearer make a particular inference over another? This question moves us away from a cognitive account of what people actually do, and instead towards considering the kinds of (potential) inferences that are *licensed* by a given sentence when it is uttered in context. Such a question is typically addressed by normative accounts that stem from commitment-based approaches to communication, championed by Hamblin (1970), Brandom (1994), Geurts (2019), and many others. There are many kinds of inferences that may be licensed by an utterance. These include the conventional meanings of words and sentences as they are produced, but can also extend to other kinds of meanings that are derivable from the uttered sentence, including entailments, presuppositions, and even implicitly communicated implicatures (see Section 3 for an overview of normative commitment accounts).

Of course, there is a difference between what may be *inferable* from a given utterance, and what is intended to be *communicated* by the speaker. Indeed, the vast array of potential inferences that are available from a given utterance will unlikely coincide one-to-one with the set of inferences that the speaker intended the hearer to recover. Nor will the set of potential inferences perfectly align with the set of inferences that the hearer *actually* recovers, whether or not the speaker intended them to do so. Since as analysts we do not have direct access to speakers' actual mental states, one way to study the inferences that interlocutors make is to observe recipients' responses as evidence for the ways in which they have understood themselves and others. This is the approach of work in talk-in-interaction and Conversation Analysis that centralises the responses of others in the 'interactional achievement' of understandings (Schegloff 1981; see Section 2 for further detail). On this approach, meanings are not tied to individual utterances or to individual speakers' intentions. Rather, meanings are viewed as intersubjective (shared between people) and emergent (can change over time) as interaction progresses.

Conversation Analysis tends to preclude theorisation about language; however, the insights that it offers by observing on-record interaction can be considered alongside both cognitive accounts and normative accounts to see whether the inferences that may be licensed by a given utterance are, indeed, the ones that participants appear to actually infer. As we progress through this Element, we will see the benefits of developing a hybrid account of pragmatic inference that encompasses speakers' intentions in the attribution of meaning, alongside accounts of objectively available meanings, both by what is inferable by the uttered sentence, as well as by the on-record ways in which speakers and hearers orient themselves to different meanings in interaction.

1.2 The Scope of the Study of Pragmatic Inference – For Now

We can study inferences as products, namely inferences as meanings derived, or at least derivable, from what is said; or we can study inferences as processes, whether cognitive, logical, or normative, and, as summarised by Terkourafi (2021), different inferential processes can lead to the same product, while the same process can lead to different products. In this Element, we will look at the study of inferences-as-products under three different, albeit interrelated, guises. Inferences can be studied as, first, the intentions of the speaker that the hearer ought to, assuming communication to be functioning as it should, infer; second, the potential inferences that are licensed by a given sentence or utterance, for example entailments and presuppositions, as well as normative conventional meanings, that may or may not be entertained by speakers but are nevertheless justifiably inferable; and third, the inferences that hearers actually make regarding a speaker's meaning, which may or may not align with the meaning that the speaker intended to communicate. We will also see how all of these inference products can be pursued via different inferential processes: the cognitive processes through which hearers entertain and 'pick' the inferences they make; the a priori logical inferential processes qua relations (e.g. entailment relations) that yield different inferential outputs; or the ways in which speakers make available inferences from what they say.

It is clear from the outset that the kinds of inferences that fall in the remit of one's area of study will depend on the perspective that the analyst takes. While we can follow a broadly Gricean approach and focus on inferences about the speaker's intended meaning, we may also acknowledge that hearers can draw all kinds of inferences from speakers' utterances that the speaker did not intend to communicate. This of course occurs in straightforward cases of misunderstanding, such as if a hearer misheard or misinterpreted what the speaker said, or if the speaker miscommunicated their intended meaning, for example through 'slips of the tongue' or mispronunciations. As these kinds of cases evidence 'faulty' communication, they may appear to be of little interest to a theory of communication that aims to describe and explain how communication works when things go as they should. However, as we will explore throughout this Element, inferences lie on a cline from clearly intended to clearly unintended, and disputes over what was said or what was meant can be very important to a theory of communication: they provide evidence for the kinds of meanings that are inferable from different kinds of utterances, and they demonstrate where potential problems in communication can lie. They can also be important to speakers themselves as they work with their conversational partners to figure out their joint attitudes towards relevant issues, or to avoid responsibility for inferences attributed to them but that they didn't mean to communicate.

So, although different scholarly accounts may ask different questions and take different kinds of evidence as input, looking at the different theoretical options on offer – and note that we will only highlight a handful here – hints at how combining approaches can be fruitful for gaining a full picture of the nature of pragmatic inference as their insights inform one another. For example, as more progress is made on understanding the cognitive processing of language, more accurate developments can be made towards generalisations of normative language use that are faithful to how people actually use language, while observations about how speakers orient to certain aspects of meaning in real time can provide evidence for how speakers prioritise and structure different kinds of inferences in the mind.

Now, while pragmatic inference is typically equated with the meaning of a given utterance, it has to be recognised that people do not just communicate one single message when they speak. We already know that they can simultaneously convey explicit and implicit messages. But as we also know, it's not just *what* the speaker said that has communicative importance, it's *how* they said it, or, as we will discuss, in some cases what they *didn't* say. In addition to implicatures, presuppositions, and entailments that we have touched upon so far, there is a wealth of other types of inference that can arise in the course of linguistic communication, including inferences relating to social dynamics, attitudes, and emotions. For example, use of indirect or mitigating language can offer insights into how the speaker perceives their relationship with their interlocutor. Use of irony, sarcasm and other figurative language might indicate something about the speaker's mood or attitude. Use of slang or taboo language may invoke inferences about the speaker's emotional state. And paralinguistic cues such as tone of voice, accent, volume of speech, gestures, and facial expressions can accompany language use to help draw such inferences. All of these inferences will be 'pragmatic' in the sense that they are defeasible, although they will range in the extent to which they are intended or unintended to be communicated, or indeed consciously or subconsciously communicated.

Viewing, as Haugh (2007: 90–1) does, implication as 'anything that is the consequence of something else', and 'anything that can be anticipated or *inferred by the addressee* from what is said' (my emphasis), what is to say that the study of pragmatic inference should not extend to consider this wider array of inferences? To do so would not only go beyond the scope of pragmatic inference as the recovery of speakers' intentions in the spirit of post-Gricean pragmatics, but also beyond the joint process of co-constructing propositional meanings, or negotiating commitment for communicating propositions. It would take us further into the realm of attitudes, emotions, social propriety, and other *ways* of expressing oneself that can, in some situations, have a greater impact on communicative outcomes and interpersonal relations than the content of what is expressed. Scholars have started to consider this vast array of inferences that one can obtain from utterances that go beyond what was said or what was meant, and full consideration of how such inferences have been and can be studied will certainly take us beyond the scope of this Element. But what will hopefully become clear through this brief precis of theoretical options is that the question of where the locus of meaning lies is not only relevant to pragmatic theory, but is also of paramount importance for real-life communicative issues, including managing everyday instances of interpersonal communication conflict where 'what is said', 'what is meant', and 'what is communicated' are at issue.

2 'Faulty Inferences': Speaker Intentions, Indeterminate Meanings, and Misunderstandings

Since Grice's (1975) seminal work on the relationship between what is said and what is meant, the term 'pragmatic inference' typically refers to a hearer's understanding of a speaker's intended meaning. On this view, as long as a hearer infers a speaker's intention from their utterance, communication can proceed unhindered. But we also know that hearers can draw all kinds of inferences from a speaker's utterance that the speaker did not intend to communicate, which are usually seen to lie outside Grice's account. This section begins with an overview of Grice's distinction between 'what is said' and 'what is implicated' and the debates that followed in distinguishing these two aspects of meaning, before moving beyond Grice's account to consider different kinds of inferences that can or should be included in a pragmatic theory of communication. This involves considering issues of (in)determinacy of both utterance content and speaker intention, as well as questioning how far a hearer's inference needs to align with the speaker's intention for communication to be 'successful'.

2.1 Pragmatic Inferences and 'What Is Said'

We start here with Grice's (1957) work on non-natural meaning, 'meaning$_{NN}$', that turned its attention away from how meanings are solely derived from sentences and their component parts, and towards speaker meaning as intentional meaning. For him, for a speaker to mean$_{NN}$ something by an utterance is for the speaker to produce an utterance with the intention of inducing a belief in the hearer by having them recognise this intention (see Grice 1989: 220). A rational, cooperative speaker – abiding by the Cooperative Principle and conversational maxims – is thus expected to formulate their utterance in such a way that it would be understood by the hearer in the way the speaker intended to be understood (see Jaszczolt 2023, chapter 7 for a recent – detailed and critical – overview of Grice's work on speaker meaning).

Now, in framing meaning$_{NN}$ in terms of speakers' intentions, Grice acknowledged that 'speaker meaning' can depart from sentence meaning and what is explicitly 'said', and instead constitute a conversational implicature. For him, meaning$_{NN}$ is the composition of 'what is said' and 'what is implicated', and the study of the two have subsequently been viewed as separate enterprises. 'What is said' is typically viewed as a product of the language system as 'sentence meaning', and is considered the bearer of truth conditions. Meanwhile, 'what is implicated' is often related to 'speaker meaning', involves contextual information for its recovery, and is traditionally not considered truth-conditional. However, later theorists in the neo- and post-Gricean traditions have long noted that the dividing line is not this clear-cut, with debates abounding as to how to distinguish 'what is said' and 'what is implicated': what Horn (2006) labelled the 'border wars'.

Grice himself could be credited with paving the way for this debate in his observation that sentences underdetermine truth-conditional meaning in cases of ambiguity and reference assignment (see Grice 1978, 'Further Notes on Logic and Conversation'), and that context is necessarily required for their resolution. This observation has been extended by various theorists to other syntactically complete but semantically underdetermined sentences for which additional contextual information is required to communicate something meaningful. On such a 'contextualist' view, sentences like (1) only bear truth conditions on the supply of information from context that indicates what the speaker is not ready *for*. That is, (1) will mean something very different in a situation where the speaker is not ready *to start writing*, to the situation in which the speaker is not ready *to eat lunch*.

(1)   I'm not ready.

This process of adding contextual information has been described as 'filling in' (Bach 1994), or 'saturation' (Recanati 2004), as it involves saturating the logical form by filling in the sentence from the 'bottom up'.

There are also cases in which lexical items may need 'fleshing out' (Bach 1994) to make sense in a given context. Assuming that the referent of 'he' in (2) is a human, its utterance invites the hearer to create an 'ad hoc concept' (Carston 2002) of 'snake' by drawing on the relevant features of snakes that the referent shares, leading the hearer of the utterance to infer the likely intended meaning that the person in question is devious in some way.

(2)   He's a snake.

This kind of 'top down' 'free enrichment' (Carston 2002) or 'modulation' (Recanati 2010) of the logical form is not linguistically mandated insofar as it can be *possible* to obtain a fully fledged truth-conditional proposition from the uttered sentence. However, in seeking truth conditions that reflect the ways in which speakers use and understand their utterances, scholars of a 'contextualist' orientation take the view that such pragmatic inferences should be used to enrich the logical form of the sentence to generate a unit of 'what is said' that outputs truth conditions in line with speakers' intuitions about them. Recanati (2004, 2010) goes so far as to argue that – while his pragmatic operation of modulation is an optional, context-dependent process – *no* truth-evaluable unit is free from pragmatic inferencing.

There is ample debate over which kinds of meanings are generated by bottom up versus top down processes, including but not limited to the domain of quantifier expressions (e.g. restricting the domain of 'every' in 'every bottle is empty' to those on the table or at the party; see Stanley and Szabó 2000), narrowed readings of logical connectives (e.g. taking 'and' to mean 'and then' or 'and as a result', see Carston 1988, 2002), and strengthened concepts encoded by lexical items (e.g. our 'snake' example above, see again Carston 2002). Likewise, how far we go with allowing context to intrude on the logical form of the uttered sentence depends on one's theoretical commitments. While as we've seen Relevance Theory and Recanati equate 'what is said' with their own versions of enriched logical forms, other theorists (e.g. Jaszczolt 2005, 2010) go right to the end of the spectrum in prioritising the study of semantics with the *main*, 'primary', meaning that a speaker intended, which may adhere to the logical form of the utterance to varying degrees, in some cases overriding it altogether to encompass an implicitly communicated implicature. Others allow 'what is said' to encompass a co-constructed, or interactionally achieved, meaning between all discourse participants (e.g. Elder and Haugh 2018, Elder 2019), which again can reflect the logical form to different degrees depending on how the participants themselves understand that meaning.

While it is not our aim to resolve these debates here, together they highlight that the scope of the study of pragmatic inference is not limited to recovering conversational implicatures as aspects of meaning that go beyond 'what is said'. Inferential work is equally needed for the recovery of meanings that are communicated to different degrees of explicitness via the sentence form itself, which involve both bottom up and top down contextual intrusion. Top down inferences are more 'pragmaticky' than bottom up ones in the sense that they are not mandated by the sentence itself, but other contextual considerations. But even if one postulates covert 'slots' in the logical form to be filled in bottom up by information from context, it is the job of the hearer to use relevant information from the context in order to fill those slots and recover the appropriate meaning. So, it is not that any interpretation 'will do', but that the meaning that is intended to be recovered by the hearer is systematically constrained by both the linguistic system and the available contextual information, and it is the task of the hearer to combine relevant pieces of linguistic and extra-linguistic information in order to arrive at a contextually relevant interpretation of the speaker's utterance.

As to the debate on how much context can intrude on the logical form of the uttered sentence, and hence where to draw the line between 'what is said' and 'what is implicated', one option for a guiding principle is to consider the nature of pragmatic inferences as cognitive processes. Recanati (2004), for example, distinguishes 'primary pragmatic processes' from 'secondary pragmatic processes', and these he argues are responsible for the recovery of 'what is said' and 'what is implicated', respectively. For Recanati, 'primary pragmatic processes' are automatic, subconscious, and based on associative mechanisms in the brain. They are responsible for both saturation of linguistically mandated elements of the sentence (such as reference assignment to indexicals), as well as the optional, top-down process of modulation that is not enforced by the linguistic expression, but which nevertheless contributes to generating a truth-conditional meaning that aligns with the speaker's intuitions. But crucially, they do not involve actually *reflecting* on the speaker's intended meaning; primary pragmatic processes are 'as direct as perception' (Recanati 2002). It is 'secondary pragmatic processes', by contrast, that he considers to be truly 'inferential'. They are controlled, consciously available, and involve reasoning about the speaker's rationality, beliefs and intentions. These inferential processes are the ones that are responsible for generating implicatures, that is, aspects of meaning that are distinct from the logical form of the sentence.

While this distinction offers us a neat dividing line for the division of labour between semantics and pragmatics, it relies on key assumptions regarding the nature of cognitive processing. Mazzone (2018) aligns with Recanati (and other definitions in psychology) in taking inferential processes to be 'characterized by conscious attention and sustained activation' (Mazzone 2018: 71). Like Recanati, he also posits pre-inferential processes stemming from associative mechanisms: different kinds of associative networks in working memory that are activated by an utterance. But where Mazzone comes apart from Recanati is that associative mechanisms can be either automatic (subconscious) or controlled (conscious). Moreover, Mazzone postulates that conscious inferential processes (that are implemented by associative mechanisms) can be responsible for activating both explicit and implicit meanings. The upshot is that we no longer have a neat dividing line between automatic and controlled processes corresponding to the processes responsible for 'what is said' and 'what is implicated', respectively.

There is also a key terminological issue to be addressed regarding the nature of inferential processes. While Recanati and Mazzone use the term 'inferential processes' to refer to those that are consciously controlled, Relevance Theory uses the term 'inferential' to encompass the domain of pragmatic processes more broadly. Indeed, they term their theoretical endeavour as 'doing inferential pragmatics', the goal of which 'is to explain how the hearer infers the speaker's meaning on the basis of the evidence provided' (Wilson and Sperber 2004: 607). In this sense, all utterance processing is 'inferential' insofar as it involves the rational construction of an inference from the speaker's utterance and contextual assumptions, resulting in a warranted conclusion regarding the speaker's intended meaning via the process of satisfying the hearer's expectation of relevance (see e.g. Wilson and Carston 2006). This inferential processing is automatic, not necessarily consciously available, and applies to both 'what is said' (in Relevance Theory terminology: 'explicatures') and 'what is implicated'.

Mazzone does note that his way of viewing inferential processes does not preclude using the term 'inferential' to describe the subconscious, automatic processes of the mind in the way that Relevance Theory does. As he says, 'pragmatic processes can be said to be inferential in Grice's sense provided that they admit of a rational reconstruction, irrespective of the actual processes by which they are implemented' (Mazzone 2018: 72). In this sense, associative mechanisms can 'perform inferences' to the extent that it is possible for those processes to be rationally constructed. But note that 'rational construction' should not be conflated with 'conscious construction'; a rationally constructed inference is one that can be reasonably and logically derived from given premises, while reference to consciousness is a psychological concern that cross-cuts the issue of rationality.

It is in this broader sense that this Element refers to inferential processes as we move forward: without taking a stance on the actual cognitive mechanisms of the mind, we can assume that some pragmatic processing (whether inferential or not, depending on one's definition) is consciously constructed, while some is automatic and subconscious. Furthermore, it remains up for debate whether, and if so how, cognitive processing can help us distinguish meanings of different kinds of explicitness. The next section steps away from this debate, and highlights that when we look at the kinds of meanings that can be considered explicit or implicit, the line dividing such meanings may not be so clear cut after all.

2.2 Indeterminate Intentions and Faulty Inferences

Viewing pragmatic inference as the successful recovery of speaker intentions is not as straightforward as it seems for the simple reason that recovering speakers' intended meanings is not always a clear-cut task. On the one hand, hearers are charged with the tricky business of sifting relevant clues from the wealth of contextual information available to them in order to arrive at a plausible conclusion as to what the speaker intended to communicate. But further challenges abound in the face of potentially indeterminate speaker meanings. As highlighted by Sperber and Wilson (2015), speaker meanings lie on a continuum from fully propositional determinate meanings at one end, to indeterminate meanings that are not uniquely paraphrasable at the other. For example, poetic metaphors such as (3) do not yield a single, unique proposition that constitutes *the* intended meaning of the expression, and nor ought they; as they say, 'the communicator's meaning cannot be paraphrased without loss' (Sperber and Wilson 2015: 122).

(3)   Juliet is the sun.

The upshot is that, as Wilson and Sperber (2002) argue, the amount of pragmatic inferencing required to recover an explicature from a single utterance will also vary depending on how far the explicature – as a developed logical form – departs from the uttered linguistic form, with explicit messages generally requiring less processing effort than implicit ones.

Subsentential speech provides a ripe testing ground for issues of determinacy, as sources of information for filling in missing constituents can range from clear-cut copy-paste cases of syntactic ellipsis, to indeterminate cases requiring more extensive pragmatic inferencing (Savva 2017). In (4), the speakers are talking about their mutual friends, Karen and Ian. Speaker A responds to B's syntactically incomplete conditional structure 'if he has good rates . . . ' in line 4 with 'that's true' in line 5. But determining what exactly speaker A deems to be 'true' is elusive in the absence of a fully propositional conditional form due to the trailed off utterance in the previous turn.

(4)   1   A   And Karen and Ian want to buy her half of the mortgage out, so
                  they'll have too much mortgage
         2   B   Yeah . . . it really is . . .
         3   A   I know. With Ian only a tennis coach
         4   B   Well even now. I mean, **if he has good rates, good bank rates, and
                  he's got a steady job** . . .
         5   A   That's true.

(ICE-GB: S1A-036, 035; discussed in Elder and Savva 2018)

Elder and Savva (2018) propose that a hearer could 'fill in' the missing content with a range of possible completions, including, for example: 'he could afford to pay the mortgage', 'he shouldn't worry about it', 'I think he'll be okay', and so forth. But in whatever way – or even *if* – the hearer filled in the missing consequent, it is likely that none of these options was precisely and determinately intended by the speaker, in the sense of the speaker having a clear and determinate a priori meaning intention (cf. Haugh 2008; Terkourafi 2014, among others). But if speakers need not have determinate meaning intentions, what is the object to be inferred by hearers?

The solution offered by Relevance Theory retains speaker intentions as an explanatory tool, but in a way that accords with the idea that speakers can communicate indeterminate meanings. Namely, for indeterminate expressions that do not give rise to a unique paraphrase that corresponds to the full import of the speaker's intended meaning, Sperber and Wilson (2015) argue that the speaker makes manifest an *array* of propositions that is compatible with the explicit content (the 'explicature'). Crucially, no single one of these options is, or should be, the unique proposition attributable to the speaker's intended meaning, but together they communicate a relevant *impression* that the hearer can recover.

This potential indeterminacy of utterance meanings leads Wilson (2018) to emphasise a difference between 'comprehension', recognising the intended import of an utterance, and 'interpretation', drawing conclusions about what was communicated. As she says,

> When the intended import consists of a wide array of propositions, there may be no clear cut-off point between comprehension and interpretation. While some propositions in the array will be strongly communicated (in the sense that the communicator made it strongly manifest that she intended to make these specific propositions manifest), others may be more weakly communicated, so that an addressee who decides to accept them must take some responsibility for

their truth. As communication becomes weaker, comprehension shades off into interpretation, and communication is no longer a yes–no matter but a matter of degree. (Wilson 2018: 189)

Elder and Savva (2018) take a similar tack, arguing that in the case of subsentential speech, even if a speaker does not have a particular completion in mind that would yield a fully fledged proposition, admissible completions are expected to be members of a set of propositions that overlap in their pragmatic implications. So as long as the hearer is able to recover relevant content that is *compatible* with what the speaker could plausibly have intended, there is no detriment to communication as long as the interlocutors are aligned at the level of the main message communicated, and hence what constitutes an appropriate response (cf. Elder 2019).

The challenges of considering pragmatic inference as the successful recovery of speakers' intentions do not stop there. In some cases, the speaker *may* have a determinate completion in mind, and how recoverable this is will depend on the specific context of utterance. But in other cases, it may be that the speaker deliberately leaves the interpretation of their utterance open without having a clear-cut intention in mind as to what should be recovered, thereby offering the hearer some freedom in continuing the interaction in a way that suits them. For example, as Haugh (2011) discusses, when a speaker utters (5), the ellipsis site leaves open whether the disjunction functions as a polar question ('would you like coffee *or not*'), or as an alternative question ('would you like coffee *or something else*'), itself leaving open to the hearer to request alternative drinks (e.g. tea, beer) or even an alternative activity (see also Jaszczolt et al. 2016 for discussion of the '*p* or . . . ' construction).

(5)   Would you like a coffee or . . . ?

Such a rhetorical move is labelled by Clark (1997: 588) as an 'elective construal', where 'speakers deliberately offer their addressees a choice of construals, so when addressees make their choice, they help determine what the speaker is taken to mean'. That is, the hearer is not simply required to recover *the* intended meaning of the speaker, but the speaker's indeterminate use of the language in the first place *licenses* the hearer to recover one of several available potential inferable meanings. Terkourafi (2014: 53–4) calls this 'enabling': the hearer 'amplifies' the speaker's meaning, going 'beyond the speaker's intention yet still in a direction ratified by [the speaker]':

In this way, she [the speaker] makes him [the hearer] an accomplice in the inferential process, inviting him to share with her the responsibility of figuring out the full set of implications of her statement. (Terkourafi 2014: 56)

Insofar as we move away from an account of utterance meaning and towards one of communication more broadly, a question arises regarding the extent to which hearers' inferences do, or need to, align with speakers' intentions in order for communication to progress smoothly. Assuming linguistic forms to under-determine utterance content, it is inevitable that speakers and hearers will not come to perfectly aligned shared representations of what is said. That is, utterance processing inevitably leads to constant micro-misalignments between interlocutors. However, rather than considering these misalignments to be a problem for communication, one can consider them as beneficial if they contribute to a process of information growth or increased common ground (see Elder and Beaver 2022 on this point).

To illustrate, consider the following light-hearted example from the animated movie, *Ratatouille*. In this movie, Remy is a rat with a self-proclaimed excellent sense of smell and a passion for cooking. Remy and his brother Emile are rummaging around in a human's kitchen looking for ingredients.

(6) 1 Remy I'm telling you, saffron will be just the thing. Gusteau swears by it.
2 Emile Okay, who's Gusteau?
3 Remy Just the greatest chef in the world! He wrote this cookbook. (A copy of Auguste Gusteau's 'Anyone Can Cook!' is revealed)
4 Emile W- w- w- wait. You ... read?
5 Remy Well, not excessively.
6 Emile Oh man. Does dad know?

(*Ratatouille*, 2007, Pixar Animation Studios. Film)

Emile's question 'you read?' in line 4 ostensibly asks Remy about his ability to read, an interpretation that is strongly inferable given that Remy is a rat, and hence is not expected to be able to read. Remy's response 'not excessively' communicates the strong implicature that he reads somewhat often. What is of interest here is that Remy's response actually answers a subtly different question to the one we presume Emile to have asked: it responds to a question about Remy's habitual activities. Remy's response therefore reveals a mismatch between his interpretation of Emile's question, and Emile's presumed intention in his asking of that question.

But note that this mismatch is not a problem for Emile. In answering the unintended habitual question, Remy also reveals his ability to read (insofar as a prerequisite for reading occasionally is an ability to read), thereby implicitly giving a positive answer to Emile's intended question. In this respect, Remy actually offers more information than was asked for, both divulging that he is able to read, as well as indicating the frequency with which he reads. So, Emile's presumably unintentionally ambiguous question actually results in greater alignment vis-à-vis the answer to his initial question, even though there is a seeming misalignment between Remy and Emile regarding what the intended question was. That is, in providing Emile with more information than he initially asked for, the two interlocutors are more greatly aligned than they would have been had Remy answered Emile's putative intended meaning.

Now, even if we allow for such misalignments between speakers and hearers in the purview of 'successful communication', again, it is not that there are *no* constraints on hearer interpretations. Indeed, it can matter a lot to speakers whether they are understood in the way they intended to be understood. So the question is: how far can we go in allowing hearer interpretations to diverge from speaker intentions without detriment to the overall communicative endeavour?

In addition to 'elective construals' discussed above, Clark (1997) goes a step further to identify what he terms 'accepted misconstruals'. This is a more radical step away from the Gricean programme, as it allows patent misunderstandings a legitimate place in normative communicative practices. Accepted misconstruals are where 'speakers present an utterance with one intention in mind, but when an addressee misconstrues it, they change their minds and accept the new construal' (Clark 1997: 589). In such cases, the hearer's inference leads the speaker to update their own conception of how their previous utterance has been interpreted, and allows the new interpretation to guide the future discourse. The interaction in (7) is reported by Clark as having occurred between him and a server while he was ordering a drink in a cafe.

(7)   1   Server   And what would you like to drink?
       2   Clark   Hot tea, please. Uh, English breakfast.
       3   Server   That was Earl Grey?
       4   Clark   Right.

(Clark 1997: 589)

The misunderstanding in this example hinges on the information that Earl Grey tea is a different kind of tea to English Breakfast tea (and not simply an exemplar of English tea that is typically drunk at breakfast time, although this belief could explain the rationale for the server's proposal in line 3). To wit, when the server proposes 'Earl Grey?', this is a different option to the English breakfast tea Clark previously requested. What is interesting is that Clark is seen to accept the server's alternative proposal in line 4. As Clark (1997: 589) claims, 'I initially intended to be taken as meaning one thing, but I changed my mind. Speakers may accept a misconstrual because they deem it too trivial, disrupting, or embarrassing to correct. Still, once it is grounded, it is taken to be what they mean'. Through

Clark's analysis of this situation, we see that, despite recognising the server's faulty inference of his initial tea order, Clark used the server's displayed inference to update his real-world tea preferences and hence to continue the interaction as if no disfluency had occurred.

Such cases are interesting for the reason that, despite the hearer mishearing or misinterpreting the speaker's initial request, it was due to the hearer's erroneous inference that the interaction was taken down a different path to the one that the speaker had previously anticipated. Moreover, even though the hearer 'got it wrong', so to speak, their erroneous inference even turned out to be beneficial to the speaker insofar as a new option was presented that the speaker ended up finding preferable.

Once we depart from a strict adherence to pragmatic inference as being the recovery of speaker intentions, we are left in somewhat murky waters as to the kinds of inferences that have a place in a formal theory of communication. Indeed, as we move further along the line and we consider the inferences that hearers make that lie *outside* the bounds of what could plausibly have been intended by a speaker, we get into the realms of misunderstandings proper, which, according to some scholars, should not fall within the scope of a normative theory of meaning. As Jaszczolt (2012: 98) states: 'conversational breakdown and miscommunication have to, by definition, fall outside a theory of what interactants rationally do [. . .] One can have either (a) a [contextualist] semantic theory or (b) psycho- and sociolinguistic explanations of miscommunication, but not both at once'.

On the one hand, one can see that cases where a hearer's inference 'gets it wrong' are not so interesting for a normative theory of utterance meaning, if, by 'gets it wrong', we mean that there was some breakdown in the communicative channel or mismatched expectations of what was in the common ground, and therefore the inference should not have been made if communication was working as it should. But there is a case to be made for misunderstandings to be of interest to a theory of *meaning in communication* more broadly. First, we have seen that misunderstandings do not necessarily lead to 'communicative breakdown' from which speakers are unable to continue the discourse due to some gross mismatch of understandings. Second, to dub many of the examples above as 'misunderstandings' just because the speaker's intended meaning does not perfectly align with the hearer's inferred content seems too coarse, as they demonstrate expected and natural disfluencies involved in the comprehension process. And third, it is worth bearing in mind that inferring the other speaker to have 'got it wrong', so to speak, is also an inference in itself that leads to further inferences, which provides insights into the ways in which speakers negotiate meanings in interaction, in turn offering insights into the meanings that speakers activate and prioritise.

So, we move away from the question of how words and sentences combine with the context of utterance such that the hearer is able to obtain the 'correct' inference about what the speaker intended in the spirit of Gricean and post-Gricean pragmatics. Instead, we move towards a more liberal view of pragmatic inference that can account for a wider array of content that is not tied to a strict notion of speaker intention, but includes those *potential* meanings that are licensed by an utterance, as well as those meanings that are actually inferred by hearers irrespective of the speaker's intentions. But, to be clear, it is not that speaker intentions do not have a place in pragmatic theory; simply that the recovery of intentions is not *all* that is important when considering the range of inferences that are available from speakers' utterances, what Terkourafi (2021) calls the totality of 'meaning occasioned by a speaker's use of language'. As Hansen and Terkourafi (2023) argue, speaker intention is just one source among others through which hearers can make assumptions about what has been communicated. So, once we move away from the goal of looking for generalisations regarding how speakers' intentions are inferable via the interrelation of utterances and contexts, we now require some other theoretical tool(s) to study such non-intended aspects of meaning.

2.3 Equivocality of Inferences and the Role of Uptake in the Interactional Achievement of Utterance Meaning

Contravening work in the Gricean tradition that assumes pragmatic inference as intention attribution to be central to communication, it is exactly because speakers can accept divergent interpretations of what they have said through their subsequent utterances that meaning in communication might, in some cases, be better construed as that which is co-constructed (or 'co-constituted' in Arundale's 1999 terms) by speakers and hearers together, irrespective of a speaker's initial intentions. Utterances are no longer imbued with determinate content at the point of production, but instead are viewed as *inviting* hearers to respond in particular ways. Now, although work in talk-in-interaction and Conversation Analysis avoids attributing intentions as mental states to speakers on the basis of what they say, as Dynel (2016) points out, the idea of 'inferences that speakers make available from what they say' is, conceptually even if not ontologically, compatible with a notion of 'intention recognition'. As such, we could afford speakers with something like 'proto-intentions' (terminology from Terkourafi 2021): intentions that may lack full determinacy with regard to utterance meanings, whose utterances then invite hearers to help clarify what those intentions – or at least meanings communicated – might be. Or we can 'go the whole hog' and remove intentions from the explanatory toolkit altogether in the spirit of Conversation Analysis, and focus solely on the ways in which speakers display their inferences through their on-record utterances, without any speculation on speakers' mental states.

Whichever route we go vis-à-vis speaker intentions, to account for pragmatic inference in this now wider sense, it seems that a fruitful way forward is to give hearer responses greater priority in the study of pragmatic inference by the way in which they evidence how speakers 'operationalise' (Arundale 2013) utterance meanings together, as well as how those responses shape the future discourse. We have already seen that speakers do not always produce perfectly fully fledged grammatical sentences. But rather than tasking hearers with the job of 'filling in' missing constituents that are attributed to the speaker's intention, in looking at the hearer's response to the utterance, we can think of meaning generation as a broader enterprise involving a process of co-construction between multiple speakers.

The context of (8) is that the participants are sewing a pillow. In line 1, the daughter produces a partial structure that is left open to the hearer to comprehend.

(8)   1   Daughter   Oh here dad (0.2) a good way to get those corners out
                      (0.2)
       2   Dad   is to stick yer finger inside.
       3   Daughter   <u>well</u>, that's one way.

(Lerner 2004: 231)

As discussed by Gregoromichelaki et al. (2011), it is unlikely that the dad's continuation of the daughter's partial structure exactly aligned with the way that the daughter would have continued herself, either in form or in content. In fact, as Gregoromichelaki et al. (2011) point out, hearers can purposefully deviate from what the speaker was likely to have intended while remaining grammatically faithful to the initial partial structure; they term such responses 'hostile continuations' or 'devious suggestions'. Indeed, the daughter's 'well'-prefaced response in line 3 indicates that the dad's suggestion did, in some way, deviate from what she was going to say. But even if the dad's response did not match the daughter's preferred choice of phrasing, it does appear that he offered a proposal that aligned with the overall activity of 'getting the corners out'. To use terminology from Sanders (2015), even if they were not aligned at the level of a fully determinate 'utterance-level intention', they were nevertheless aligned at the level of their 'activity-level intentions', i.e. 'what the speaker intends the end result of the interaction or segment to be' (Sanders 2015: 481).

The idea that the meaning (or 'understanding' in Conversation Analysis terms) of a speaker's utterance will depend, at least in part, on the hearer's uptake has been well exemplified in the Conversational Analytic tradition. Heritage (1984) made an early observation in this regard in his contrast of (9), his own constructed example, with (10), an attested one, highlighting how the recipient's response can influence the way that the initial speaker's utterance is interpreted: it is conceivable that B's utterance could be interpreted as a complaint and therefore responded to as such, as in (9), or – as the actual recipient did in (10) – could be responded to as though an invitation had been made (see also Schegloff and Sacks 1973).

(9)   B   Why don't you come and <u>see</u> me sometimes
        A   I'm sorry. I've been terribly tied up lately

(constructed, Heritage 1984: 255)

(10)   B Why don't you come and <u>see</u> me some[times
      A   [I would like to

(SBL:10:12, Heritage 1984: 255)

Such pairs of examples illustrate how it is not only that speakers may have indeterminate intentions (as in the case of open-ended disjunction in (5) above), or that hearers' responses can override a speaker's initial intention (as in the tea example (7) above). But rather, as Arundale (2008: 242) puts it, '[s]peaker and recipient meanings and actions are *provisional* pending uptake and evolve continually into operative meanings and actions' (my emphasis).

Now, it is not only that the hearer's uptake helps attribute meaning to a previous speaker's utterance, but that the hearer's response – being publicly available – serves as an important resource for the initial speaker to appreciate how their prior utterance has been understood. Following a hearer's response, the initial speaker thus has an opportunity to display whether or not the hearer's understanding of their utterance aligned with their own expectations about how they would be understood. This third turn of the initial speaker thus contributes to the 'interactional achievement' of meaning in interaction as they confirm or disconfirm – explicitly or implicitly – the hearer's interpretation as appropriate in that moment. Accounts of communication that make use of the idea of 'interactional achievement' include, but are not limited to, Arundale's (1999, 2020) 'conjoint co-constituting' model, Clark's (1996) account of 'joint action', and Sanders (1987) 'strategic' theoretical model.

How the initial speaker's response can influence how a prior utterance meaning is operationalised is highlighted in the following example, discussed by Elder and Haugh (2018). Note that canonically, a speaker's response occurs in the *third* turn, namely directly after a recipient's prior response in the second turn. However, as we see in the example below, a speaker's response need not occur precisely in the third turn, and hence is more accurately termed a 'third position' response (Schegloff 1997).

Prior to this extract, Emma has been talking about needing to go out and buy some food as she doesn't have anything for dinner.

(11)	1	Emma	I had a little tiny bit- piece a fish
	2		so I don't know **I may have to go to the store** but you go ahead Betsy and
	3		phone it up I think maybe
	4	Betsy	they'll send it down
	5	Emma	ye[ah
	6	Betsy	[**can I add anything for you?**
	7	Emma	Oh honey thanks I think I'll ah let Guy go
	8	Betsy	[Yes
	9	Emma	[**Maybe (you) get some fish.**
	10	Betsy	Yes.
	11	Emma	I'll plan on that.

(adapted from Jefferson's NB:IV:2:R, available at https://ca.talkbank.org/)

As Emma has previously been talking about needing to buy some food, there are a range of meanings that could be inferable from Emma's declaration in line 2 that she 'may have to go to the store'. On the one hand, it could simply be a description of her possible future activities, communicated via the explicit content of her utterance. But thinking about implicit meanings (i.e. implicatures) that she may have intended to communicate, it is possible that her utterance aimed to function as a hint, or even an implicit request, for Betsy to order something for her. Indeed, her continuation 'you go ahead Betsy and phone it up' indicates Emma's awareness that Betsy is in the process of ordering her own food, and hence that adding something for Emma would not be too inconvenient. Based on Emma's utterance in context alongside the previous co-text, such an indirect requestive speech act would be calculable on Gricean principles, and available as a potential inference for Betsy to make.

Indeed, we do see Betsy respond in line 6 along these lines when she offers 'can I add anything for you?'. This formulation of Betsy's response precludes Emma's previous utterance as having been interpreted as a straightforward request, but keeps open the possibility that Betsy may have viewed it as a hint: an off record indirect request (Brown and Levinson 1987). However, Emma's explicit refusal of Betsy's offer in line 7 ('thanks I think I'll let Guy go') takes this possibility off the table, as it simultaneously acts as a denial of any intention Emma may have had at the time of her utterance in line 2 that she wanted Betsy to make such an offer. It is exactly Emma's 'third turn' response that provides the empirical rationale against attributing speaker intentions to individual utterances in abstraction from their position to the utterances of others.

Now suppose that Emma actually did have a private 'intention' for Betsy to make an offer of assistance at line 2. Even though we see Betsy 'take the bait' so to speak and provide such an offer, Emma is able to make available her inference both of the way that Betsy understood her prior utterance in line 2, but moreover, how Emma is operationalising the meaning of her own utterance in line 2, namely, of *not* having had any such intention. It is both the formulation of her initial 'hinting' utterance in line 2, coupled with her refusal in line 7, that provide Emma with plausible deniability that she did, in fact, want Betsy to make the offer in the first place (see Section 4 for further discussion on deniability). This equivocality of Emma's potential intentions at the point of utterance in line 2 leads Haugh (2017) to suggest that 'hinting' utterances of this sort are better termed 'prompts' of offers.

Note that the aim of looking at the third turn is not to simply 'check' whether a given speaker got it 'right' or not. Rather, by observing how speakers respond to one another in real time can provide useful insights into how speakers negotiate the meanings that have been communicated, in turn providing greater insights into how participants' private inferences are displayed to others. While the third position response provides the initial speaker with an opportunity to confirm or disconfirm their recipient's understanding as displayed in second position, one must be wary of retrospectively attributing an intention to the initial speaker at the time of their first turn utterance. This is for the two reasons that, first, as we know, speakers can change their minds over the course of an interaction, and in this respect, speakers' intentions vis-à-vis communicative goals can also change; and second, that utterance meanings can be negotiated over more turns beyond the third position response. Indeed, we see such an 'intention shift' in line 9 from Emma when she requests 'Maybe (you) get some fish'. So, rather than suggesting that speaker intentions – as they are tied to individual utterances – become apparent over time as an interaction unfolds, it is preferable to suggest that it is *meanings* that emerge over time: meanings that are intersubjective and interactionally achieved between participants.

This is the view of Elder and Haugh (2018), who merge a post-Gricean view on utterance meaning with the interactional achievement account in their model of conversational inferencing. They take 'speaker meaning' to be the main, primary meaning not necessarily as it is intended by the speaker at the point of utterance, but as it is eventually interactionally achieved between participants. In so doing, 'speaker meaning' is a broader concept than the familiar Gricean one in that it involves speakers and hearers converging on meanings together.

One result of viewing speaker meaning in this way is that the meaning that was putatively 'intended' at the point of utterance can get 'lost' on the conversational record. Elder and Haugh acknowledge this by including both speakers' private, intentional meanings alongside the publicly available ones in their model. This work has been developed by Elder and Jaszczolt (forthcoming) who propose the notion of a 'flexible functional proposition' as a unit of analysis that can be used to represent utterance meanings at different points of an interaction – from the point of utterance to the final interactionally achieved one – as they are co-constructed on the fly by participants.

To finish this section, it has to be acknowledged that allowing recipient uptake to contribute to the co-construction of meaning has potentially undesirable ramifications if the uptake construes the previous speaker's turn in ways that it was not intended. Discussions in the philosophy of language on 'discursive injustice' debate how recipient uptake influences the illocutionary success of a previous speaker, especially in cases where the speaker belongs to an underprivileged group. Here, scholars discuss cases of women refusing sexual encounters being interpreted as invitations; of employees of female bosses treating orders as mere requests; and of members of the LGBTQ+ community or ethnic minorities being dismissed for calling out homophobic or racist comments, respectively (see e.g. Langton 1993; Kukla 2014; Bianchi 2021).

Kukla (2014) argues that recipient uptake amounts to the original speech act constituting whatever it is portrayed as: what she calls 'uptake distortion'. For example, treating an order as a request results in the initial speech act *being* a request. While this proposal aligns with the interactional achievement account described above, as Bianchi (2021: 186) points out, 'such proposals have the dangerous consequence that a speaker may fail to perform a speech act only because her addressee is inattentive, incompetent or biased'. Langton (1993) takes a slightly different approach, arguing that a speech act without appropriate uptake suffers 'illocutionary disablement': it is as if no speech act has been made. But again, as pointed out by various scholars, if an unsuccessful refusal amounts to no refusal, a sexual perpetrator is rid of responsibility.

Such societal consequences lead Bianchi (2021) to make a case for retaining speaker intentions in an account of communication: as long as a speaker makes their intentions clear via the standard conventions for issuing a given speech act, they have fulfilled their communicative responsibilities and have successfully performed that speech act. But for Bianchi, successful performance does not amount to successful communication: if a recipient fails to respond in a way commensurate with that speech act, it is the recipient who is responsible for the communicative failure: 'what a competent, attentive, and unbiased addressee would take as a refusal is a refusal – even if the man fails to recognize it' (Bianchi 2021: 188).

2.4 The Purview of Pragmatic Theory

In assuming that successful communication relies on hearers satisfactorily inferring meanings that align with speakers' intended meanings, Grice's work did not address the questions of how or why hearers may infer meanings which were *not* intended by the speaker. This section has offered different kinds of examples extending the Gricean account to highlight that (a) speakers' intentions can range in determinacy, and hence (b) it is not always a clear-cut task for a hearer to recognise a speaker's intention, but moreover (c), successful communication does not necessarily rest on the notion of a hearer successfully and completely inferring a speaker's fully fledged intended propositional meaning.

As normative theories of meaning are concerned with what speakers 'should' do, they are not typically concerned with individual instances of when speakers 'get it wrong'. But such accounts are prone to taking a coarse view of misunderstanding that is equated with hearers' 'faulty' inferences about what a speaker said or meant. The latter half of this section has thus presented a range of examples demonstrating that misunderstanding is a gradable phenomenon that is not simply limited to a hearer failing to recover a speaker's intended meaning. This is because a hearer can recover messages that do not strictly align with what the speaker had in mind – possibly because the speaker didn't even have a specific meaning in mind – but could still be accepted by the speaker. So, rather than dubbing such fuzzy cases as 'misunderstandings' and viewing inferences as one-off products that are recoverable from single utterances, utterance meanings can instead be viewed as flexible products that are dependent on previous inferences that have been made, and future inferences that will be made. So, what might typically be written off as outside the scope of a normative theory of communication as a 'misunderstanding' can actually be seen as a natural and expected part of the communicative process.

The above notwithstanding, it goes without saying that 'genuine' misunderstandings do occur insofar as speakers can have strong beliefs about what they did or did not intend to communicate, and these can differ significantly from recipients' understandings – or indeed displays of understandings – of speakers' utterances. As such, removing intentions from the explanatory toolkit altogether loses an important distinction between intended and unintended inferences that is not only of theoretical interest but can have real-life repercussions. This is the topic of the next section: even if speakers' intentions are not always responsible for directing future discourse, the way they are conceived both theoretically and by participants themselves can have knock-on effects for the meanings that speakers are held committed to or accountable for.

3 Commitment and Accountability

Section 2 questioned the extent to which intentions should be foregrounded as the input to the study of pragmatic inference as it reflects meaning in communication. This section now extends the discussion in view of the meanings that a speaker is held committed to or accountable for. Of course speakers themselves will have beliefs about what they say – and what they don't say – and appealing to intentions is an intuitive way of delineating the meanings that a speaker could, or should, be held responsible for. Looking at issues of commitment and accountability flips the object of study on its head: rather than starting with speaker intentions to inform which meanings fall under our remit of study, issues of commitment and accountability tell us more about the meanings that are available to speakers, and moreover the meanings that are important to speakers, which in turn can guide us in the question of which meanings ought to be captured by a theory of communication that reflects cognitive reality.

In the previous section, we started with Grice's observation that speaker meaning often departs from what is 'said' through the uttered sentence, moving to the role of pragmatic inference in recovering intended utterance meanings. The resulting discussion thus stuck rather closely to considering the main, primary messages – even if indeterminately intended or communicated – that arise from speakers' utterances, whether they be the intuitive meanings as intended by the speaker, or the interactionally achieved meanings that are co-constructed between discourse participants. However, it goes without saying that neither speakers nor hearers have only single messages in mind when they communicate: even if there is one main, primary intended message that is communicated by an utterance, there will also be a host of other 'secondary' messages that speakers may communicate by the same utterance, and these can vary in the degree to which they are intended, or even the level of consciousness with which they are communicated. Moreover, speakers can say things they didn't mean, with or without conscious awareness, and hearers can infer aspects of meaning that the speaker didn't intend. So here, we start to address the questions: can a speaker be committed to a meaning they intended but a hearer failed to recover? Or can a speaker be held committed to a meaning that a hearer inferred but the speaker didn't intend?

This section looks at three accounts which view 'commitment' and 'account-ability' in different ways: the 'inferential' account of Relevance Theory that holds speakers committed to the truth of what they say as it is inferred by hearers; normative commitment-based accounts of communication by which speakers are normatively committed to the content of what they say; and interactional achievement accounts that take recipient responses as evidence for the understandings to which speakers are held 'normatively accountable'. Together, these accounts offer complementary ways of considering these two questions, and moreover, different insights regarding the kinds of meanings that are inferable in the process of communication.

3.1 Relevance Theory and Commitment

First, as discussed at length in the previous section, speakers' messages can be indeterminate in content. As the final note in his seminal paper 'Logic and Conversation', Grice (1975) himself put this indeterminacy down to the fact that single utterances can each communicate a plethora of implicatures:

> [...] since there may be various possible specific explanations, a list of which may be open, the conversational implicatum in such cases will be [a] disjunction of such specific explanations; and if the list of these is open, the implicatum will have just the kind of indeterminacy that many actual implicata do in fact seem to possess. (Grice 1989: 40)

Relevance Theorists have long considered this observation, noting further that how determinate an implicature is a matter of degree, with determinacy of implicatures lying on a cline from strong to weak. For them, 'strong implicatures' are those that are determinate in content and clearly intended to be communicated by the speaker; 'weak implicatures' are those that are more indeterminate in content and left to the hearer to recover.

In their early work, Sperber and Wilson (1986/1995) gave the example of (12), highlighting the variety of meanings that Mary's utterance might communicate.

(12)   Peter   Would you drive a Mercedes?
         Mary   I wouldn't drive ANY expensive car.

         (Sperber and Wilson 1986/1995: 194)

As they noted, Mary's utterance communicates the strong implicature that she wouldn't drive a Mercedes (via the 'implicated premise' that a Mercedes is an expensive car). But there are also weaker implicatures that Peter might infer, such as that Mary wouldn't drive a Rolls Royce or a Cadillac (on the assumed premises that these are also expensive cars), or weaker still, that Mary disapproves of displays of wealth. As they suggest, Mary would not necessarily expect Peter to recover these weak implicatures, nor are they presumed to be certainly intended by Mary. But Mary's utterance may encourage Peter to think along these lines, and hence to derive such conclusions.

Now, Relevance Theorists have also long argued that speakers are committed to the truth of what they are understood to mean by hearers (unless otherwise indicated, see Sperber and Wilson 2002: 626; Boulat 2015), giving hearers' recovered meanings precedence in determining explicatures. In this sense, speakers are *held committed* to meanings by hearers. Given that speakers' utterances can give rise to such a range of strongly and weakly communicated messages, two questions immediately follow. First, to which meanings do hearers hold speakers committed? And second, to what extent can a hearer hold a speaker committed to these different kinds of meanings?

In their early work, Sperber and Wilson began to address these questions in the following discussion:

> An utterance with a fully determinate implicated premise or conclusion forces the hearer to supply just this premise or conclusion and attribute it to the speaker as part of her beliefs. [. . .] Clearly, the weaker the implicatures, the less confidence the hearer can have that the particular premises or conclusions he supplies will reflect the speaker's thoughts, and this is where the indeterminacy lies. (Sperber and Wilson 1986/1995: 199–200)

Since then, more recent scholarship has further probed the two questions of which meanings hearers hold speakers committed to, as well as how confident a hearer can be in their assessment of the speaker's commitment to these different kinds of meanings. Moeschler (2013) offers a theoretical account of commitment based on both strength and accessibility of inference. He argues that entailments and presuppositions cannot be denied without contradiction, and hence a speaker must be more committed to their truth than to implicitly communicated content. But while being semantically 'strong', entailments and presuppositions are typically backgrounded information, so a hearer would not be expected to evaluate them. Explicatures are most accessible (as they are foregrounded and explicit), followed by implicatures (foregrounded and implicit).

We can conclude from Moeschler's summary that a hearer is likely to hold a speaker more committed to an explicature (being both accessible and explicit) than to implicatures, while a hearer would not entertain a speaker's commitment to entailments and presuppositions due to their backgroundedness. This conclusion is supported by Morency et al. (2008) who argue that it is commitment attribution (i.e. by the hearer) that is of value to meaning construction, arguing that hearers can be more confident in a speaker's explicit meaning than in their implicit ones. Mazzarella et al. (2018: 18) operationalise commitment slightly differently but still from a hearer perspective as 'a function of the direct and reputational costs the sender incurs when her message is found to be false', testing participants' likelihood to trust speakers who are found to have communicated falsehoods. They found that participants were more forgiving of implicated falsehoods than of explicit or presupposed falsehoods (which were found to be treated on a par), supporting the view that speakers are held less committed to implicatures than they are to explicit meanings; this finding has been corroborated for assertions by Yuan and Lyu (2022).

3.2 Commitments, Lying, and Misleading

The idea that speakers are more committed to explicit content than to implicit content aligns with the received view in the philosophical literature on the lying-misleading debate: a speaker is considered to be lying if (i) a speaker utters p and (ii) the speaker believes p to be false. There is also ample debate on whether a lie requires the speaker to have an intention to deceive, with some scholars incorporating this as a criterion in their definition of lying (e.g. Williams 2002), and other scholars arguing against such a requirement, for example on the basis that one can lie in the knowledge that the audience will not believe the lie. Scholars have suggested alternative criteria to lying requiring an intention to deceive, such as that the speaker 'warrants the truth of p' (is in a context where the speaker guarantees the truth of p, and not in a make-believe situation; see e.g. Carson 2010; Saul 2012), or that the speaker proposes to make p common ground (e.g. Stokke 2013, 2018) (see Mahon 2016; Meibauer 2018 for more detailed overviews on the definition of lying). In any case, what is typical of such definitions of lying is that if a speaker (knowingly) produces a *true* statement with an intention to deceive, they are not considered to be lying. However, it remains contentious whether false implicatures – even if used to deceive – are considered lies.

One of the motivations for maintaining a lying-deceiving distinction is that it can explain why it is only in cases of deceiving with a true statement, that is, of intentionally producing false implicatures, that speakers can consistently deny that they only 'said' – or 'meant' – the explicit content of what they uttered. Logical consistency is favoured by many theorists as essential for distinguishing lying from misleading. In that vein, Viebahn (2021) offers a definition of commitment that both prioritises consistency in denial as per the received lying-misleading distinction, while at the same time allowing for the possibility that some implicatures can be used to lie. The view of commitment that Viebahn espouses relies on the idea that commitment to some proposition p involves the speaker taking on a *justificatory responsibility*, that is, a responsibility to defend their *knowledge of p* if challenged. So, with regard to lying:

> By requiring liars to commit themselves to a proposition they believe to be false, [this notion of commitment] requires them to take on a justificatory responsibility to defend that they *know* the proposition put forward. And this justificatory responsibility, in turn, is based on the absence of consistent dismissals to challenges to justify knowledge regarding the proposition in question. (Viebahn 2021: 307, original emphasis)

The upshot of this speaker-oriented definition of commitment is that both presuppositions and implicatures can require as much justificatory responsibility from the speaker as explicit content. This is because it is possible for one's knowledge to be challenged from such types of meaning, as illustrated in (13) and (14) below (examples adapted from Viebahn 2021: 311).

(13)   A   Did you know that John owns a Mercedes?
       B   How do you know he owns a Mercedes? He might have rented one.

(14)   A   I've got tomatoes coming out of my ears.
       B   Did you really have a good crop? The last time I passed your patch it didn't look very promising.

In (13), speaker A communicates a factive presupposition in the that-clause, namely that John owns a Mercedes. In the face of B's challenge of A's knowledge of this presupposition, in order to be consistent with their initial utterance, A must be able to defend their knowledge that John owns a Mercedes. Likewise, in (14), A communicates the strong implicature that they've had a good crop of tomatoes, and hence must be able to defend their knowledge of this claim if challenged.

While Viebahn's definition of commitment allows a speaker to lie via a false implicature, as he claims, only *some* implicatures can be used to lie. Specifically, he speculates that it is only substitutive implicatures – ones where the main message communicated is intended to substitute the explicit formulation – to which speakers are committed. For example, in (14), the communicated message of 'I've had a good crop of tomatoes' is intended to override the explicit utterance content. Note that these are arguably cases of explicature, where the logical form is developed to give the speaker's intended meaning, and in this sense are not really implicatures, and hence can be considered part of what is explicitly communicated.

On the other hand, Viebahn suggests that speakers can legitimately deny 'knowing' the content of implicatures that are *additive*, that is, where the implicature is communicated in addition to the explicit content. To bolster this dichotomy, he draws on Grice's original formulations of the classic examples of implicatures, such as (15) below:

(15)　　A　Smith doesn't seem to have a girlfriend these days.
　　　　B　He has been paying a lot of visits to New York lately.

Implicature: Smith has, *or may have*, a girlfriend in New York.

(Grice 1989: 32, emphasis by Viebahn 2021: 312)

As Viebahn argues, it is exactly due to the equivocality of additive implicatures that speakers are not committed to them, as their potential denial is consistent with the explicit content of what they said. Indeed, in line with the mainstream view as described above, Viebahn's definition of commitment favours a strict lying-misleading distinction, motivated by the view that speakers can purposefully *avoid* commitment to propositions by communicating them implicitly, or even simply by adding hedges to explicitly signal their lack of certainty in the truth of – and hence their commitment to – a proposition. But his claim that speakers can lie via a false implicature is called into question when we consider that the kinds of 'implicatures' that can be used to lie may instead be considered, on a contextualist view, not implicatures proper, but explicitly communicated aspects of meaning.

In recent years, scholars have begun to empirically test ordinary people's folk intuitions on what counts as a lie. Weissman and Terkourafi (2018), for example, used Levinson's (2000) taxonomy of generalised conversational implicatures (GCIs) to test whether judgements differed according to the type of GCI. They found that false GCIs involving cardinals ('she has three children' implicates exactly three children) and repeated verb conjuncts ('he slept and slept' implicates slept for longer than usual) were considered lies, concluding that some (but not all) false implicatures can be used to lie. But note that these results can be explained on a contextualist view that the relevant GCIs could be considered part of explicit content (see also Wiegmann et al. 2021 on this point) and so, like Viebahn's results, give credence to the idea that enrichments to logical form can be used to lie.

Other studies have found that false implicatures can be considered lies when the implicature is strongly communicated by the speaker. Orr et al. (2017), for example, found that participants would evaluate the speaker to have lied via a false implicature when that implicature pertained to the main message communicated: a privileged interactional interpretation (Ariel 2002). Reins and Wiegmann (2021) likewise found that false implicatures could be considered lies depending on how strongly the speaker was held committed to that implicature. They thus propose that a definition of lying that tracks whether speakers are held committed to the content of what is communicated – where commitment to different kinds of strongly or weakly recovered inferences is a gradable, as opposed to absolute, notion – allows for these variations in intuitions as to whether explicitly or implicitly communicated content can constitute lies. So, a speaker can be held to be lying if they are held to be committed to some implicitly communicated meaning, even if the speaker attempts to deny having meant it. That is, the denial – even if logically consistent with what they 'said' – is not *plausible* (see Section 4 for further discussion on plausible deniability).

In line with these latter studies on lying, Bonalumi et al. (2020) find that recipients consider a speaker *more* committed to implicit content than to explicit content when the outcome is important to the recipient. They offer a range of scenarios to bolster this claim, focussing on the case of implicitly communicated promises. One such scenario is repeated below:

> Andrea is working on her Master's thesis and the final draft is almost done. Because Andrea is not a native English speaker, she asks another student, Jen, to proofread the draft. She asks: 'Can you help me out and check my writing? I'll have to hand in my thesis in three days'. Jen answers: 'I have some free time tomorrow'. Andrea receives the proofread document from Jen four days later, one day after her deadline. (Bonalumi et al. 2020: 13)

As Bonalumi et al. find in their study, it is not whether Jen communicated a message explicitly or implicitly that affects Andrea's attribution of commitment to Jen. Rather, it is Andrea's reliance on Jen's apparently implicitly communicated promise that affects Andrea's attribution of commitment to Jen. Interactions like the one constructed between Andrea and Jen are unlikely to take place in isolation, and it is likely that Jen's response would invoke clarification as to whether she was committing herself to the proofreading. Nevertheless, the findings of this study do point towards the general conclusion that hearers may consider speakers to be more committed to modulated content (explicatures) or even implicatures proper than to explicit content when it is of greater relevance to them.

As Bonalumi et al. (2020) point out, it is only in limited institutional situations, such as legal contexts, where explicit meaning has a privileged position. In those circumstances, definitions of lying that rely on a strict division between what is said and what is implicated may be of value. However, the emergence of studies that indicate that false implicatures can be used to lie suggests that what matters to ordinary people is not simply what a speaker did or did not explicitly say, but their intention to deceive and how strongly the recipient considered the speaker to have intended to communicate their implicature. Indeed, Yuan and Lyu (2022) corroborate the results of previous studies that speakers are more committed to implicated false promises than they are to false assertions, hypothesising that promises involve a future commitment of the speaker, whereas the defensibility of a false assertion is dependent on external information. On the basis of these results, it may be suggested that what matters is not necessarily whether the implicature was false, but the speaker's intention to deceive: if a speaker unknowingly asserts a falsehood, there is greater scope to let them 'off the hook' than if they fail to make good on a promise.

Collectively, these studies make a case in favour of viewing the meanings most important to a theory of communication as those that are strongly communicated by the speaker and recovered by the addressee. This may mean departing from the explicature as the primary bearer of truth conditions, and allowing the implicature to take centre stage, as it does in Default Semantics' 'primary meanings' (Jaszczolt 2005, 2010) where 'what is said' is allowed to constitute an implicitly communicated meaning, or in Ariel's (2002) privileged interactional interpretations, the speaker's most relevant contribution to the discourse.

At the same time, cases of so-called 'broken promises' suggest that the speaker's intention cannot always provide the guiding principle to what a speaker is committed to. If, as unlikely as it may be, Jen never intended to look at the thesis tomorrow, instead planning on relying on the deniability of the implicature, the fact that she strongly implicated that she would do so is what is important to the interlocutors. This leads us away from an intention-based account of commitment, and towards a more normative account, to which we now turn.

3.3 Normative Commitment

Rather than questioning which meanings speakers commit themselves to (in virtue of their communicative intentions), or which meanings speakers are held committed to by hearers (in virtue of hearers inferring a speaker's intention), the normative account is concerned with the question of which meanings speakers simply *are* committed to, that is, normatively committed in virtue of what they say. On this view, 'a commitment is not necessarily a belief of the participant who has it. We do not believe everything we say; but our saying it commits us whether we believe it or not' (Hamblin 1970: 264). We can extend this view to consider whether, and if so how, speakers can be considered committed to meanings that they did *not* necessarily intend to communicate, including to both explicitly uttered and implicitly communicated meanings.

Geurts (2019) develops a version of the normative account as a Gricean-inspired account of meaning that is not reliant on speakers' intentions. For him, a commitment is a state that arises via updates to the common ground, and this state is neither psychological nor epistemic. That is, while he admits that speakers inevitably do have private beliefs about their own commitments and others', he argues that a normative theory of communication should reflect the overarching goal of communication: to publicly share social commitments. Speech acts are the paradigm commitment-sharing devices, and when one produces a speech act, one commits to acting in accordance with the content of that speech act.

A commitment is defined as a relation between a speaker, hearer and a proposition p, and in order to count as a commitment, it must be accepted into the common ground by both speaker and hearer. In uttering p, the speaker is thus committed to the content of whatever speech act they have performed. Furthermore, in proposing to update the common ground with p, the speaker also undertakes any commitments that can be derived from p, including entailments, presuppositions, and implicatures. Geurts proposes that implicatures arise in the 'usual' Gricean way through principles of rationality, but, crucially, without recourse to speakers' intentions. Namely, in uttering p, a speaker implicates q assuming the following are in the common ground:

(i)   the speaker has said p;
(ii) the speaker observes Grice's maxims;
(iii) it would not be possible for the speaker to be observing the maxims unless they were committed to q;
(iv) the speaker has not done anything to prevent q from becoming common ground;
(v)   the speaker is committed to the goal that q becomes common ground.

(adapted from Geurts 2019: 21)

It is worth pointing out that Geurts uses the terms 'common ground' and 'mutual commitment' somewhat interchangeably, which may give the appearance that speakers and hearers must somehow agree on what is in the common ground. However, Geurts reminds us not to fall into this trap: just because a speaker has updated the common ground with p, does not entail that the speaker *believes p*: 'mutual commitment is a social concept, not a psychological one, and it doesn't entail belief, let alone mutual belief' (Geurts 2019: 17). In other words, a speaker can be committed to p and its derivatives without awareness of being so committed:

> Commitments are interpersonal relationships that are established in the wake of our social activities, and it is entirely possible to engage in the game of sharing and acting on commitments without knowing one's commitments or others', and indeed without knowing what commitments are. (Geurts 2019: 15)

So, rather than offering a psychological account of the meanings that speakers believe they are committed to, or that hearers hold speakers committed to, his account prioritises the set of normative commitments that arise from speakers' utterances. These commitments stem from the inferences that a hearer is *licensed* to make from an utterance of *p*, even if such inferences are not actually *entertained* by the speakers themselves. In other words, speakers are committed to any potential meanings that are available from what they say, even if the speaker had no intention to communicate them.

The idea that speakers can be committed to unintended meanings may sit uncomfortably with those speakers who are charged with such commitments. However, there is an intuitive theoretical benefit to this normative commitment account. While speakers *ought* to endorse their commitments, they may not, in reality, actually endorse them. The normative commitment account provides the theoretical rationale for why a speaker might attempt to renounce claim to their commitments, while also explaining why a hearer can legitimately hold a speaker accountable to an aspect of meaning they didn't intend to communicate, or didn't realise they communicated.

At the same time, when considering the kinds of meanings that are of potential interest to a theory of communication, there are some key objections that are important to acknowledge. First, as Harris (2019) points out, decoupling speakers' beliefs from their commitments is problematic if we are to understand undertaking social commitments as coordinating future actions with others. That is, in *not* requiring speakers to recognise what they are committed to, it is possible – in theory – for a speech act to be successfully performed in virtue of the fact that the speakers are committed to a given future action and that it is common ground (in Geurt's sense as described above) that they are so committed, but without actually recognising they are committed to that future action. Harris goes so far as to suggest that on Geurts' account, it is possible for speakers to be committed to some speech act *p* in virtue of what is said, but by some communicative mishap come to believe that they are committed to not-*p*. This leads us to a theoretical dilemma as to the object of study for a theory of communication. While there are benefits of acknowledging and observing the potential inferences available from what is said, as Harris suggests, it is surely speakers' beliefs – including their beliefs about their commitments – that are of greater interest to communication than what has been 'objectively' and theoretically committed.

Finally, in defining commitments as a three-place relation between speaker, hearer, and proposition, there is no scope for explaining misunderstandings on this account. The issue of misunderstanding is particularly pertinent when we consider that the scope of 'normative commitment' need not be limited to semantic meanings available from what is said. Rather, it can also encompass the wide array of interpersonal, social and cultural obligations that utterances may communicate, and differences in sociocultural backgrounds can result in differences regarding what counts as a 'normative commitment'. Admittedly, as also discussed in the previous section, normative accounts of communication typically aim to describe how communication occurs as it *should*, and it may be argued that the concept of normative commitment is relative to the conventions and norms of the society or culture in which it is adopted. So, there are benefits to appealing to 'objectively available' potential inferences from what is said as it offers justification for speakers' assessments when misunderstandings do arise. But we have already seen how meanings are not always determinately identifiable from what is said, which can make it difficult – both practically and theoretically – to determinately identify what commitments have been made from a given utterance.

3.4 Interactional Achievements and Normative Accountability

On the normative commitment account, speakers can, in theory, be committed to a vast array of potential messages; however, the commitments derived from speakers' utterances need not be consciously available to either speakers or hearers. Indeed, speakers and hearers *cannot* be expected to entertain all the possible inferences that are licensed by a given utterance. This raises a question of which meanings speakers and hearers do, in fact, entertain, and hence which meanings speakers and hearers come to accept as shared commitments. While we cannot suppose to get into the minds of speakers to answer this question, the interactional achievement account, as introduced in the previous section, can offer us some insight.

The interactional achievement account offers a way of observing how speakers hold one another *normatively accountable* for meanings: it is through recipients' responses that speakers are held accountable for the meanings they make available from what they say. So rather than a speaker being held committed to a meaning due to the way in which the hearer inferred the speaker's intention, or a speaker being normatively committed through the utterance itself, a speaker is held normatively accountable to a given meaning by the recipient responding in a way that is commensurate with that interpretation. That is, through their response, a recipient makes available an inference about how they have understood the previous speaker's utterance, and hence the previous speaker is held accountable for the meaning that was communicated in virtue of it having been made the object of a future utterance.

Moreover, hearers not only hold speakers accountable to what they say via their responses, but given that participants assume agency of their conversational partners, they also hold speakers accountable to what they have communicated in virtue of their having produced an utterance in a particular way at a particular moment in a particular context. This gives us a deontological notion of meaning in interaction: speakers do inevitably have beliefs about how they expect to be understood, and how their turns are employed in interaction can have real-world repercussions for them. So, in producing an utterance, a speaker makes available their own inference of how they expect that utterance to be understood, and through a process of meaning negotiation, participants can presume that the meaning that is operationalised is akin to the meaning that the utterance is expected to have in that sequential context.

Now, it is not only that speakers and hearers are not expected to entertain all the possible inferences available from what is said – i.e. all the meanings to which they are theoretically committed – but that, as Haugh (2013: 134) says, 'neither speakers nor recipients are *held accountable* for all the inferences they make when participating in interaction' (my emphasis). That is, the meanings that are privately entertained by speakers do not always make it onto the public conversational record if they are not engaged with in subsequent interaction: '[w]e can sometimes choose which inferences we draw, and perhaps more importantly, we can choose which inferences we *indicate* we have drawn to others' (Haugh 2017: 285, original emphasis). So what apparently gets 'lost' on the interactional achievement account are those inferences that are privately made but not publicly displayed. However, this view of things simplifies the situation too much: in the same way that utterance meanings can lie on a cline from determinate to indeterminate as we have seen, surely the understandings that recipient responses display can also range from explicit to equivocal of the utterances they target.

In simple cases, recipients' responses can explicitly expose inferences that have been communicated by a previous speaker, even when those inferences have been implicitly communicated.

(16)   (Chad is standing in the hallway, holding his 15-month old son's hand.)
    1   Chad   Hey, Debbie.
    2   Are you going to be free from 1:30 to 2:30?
    3   Debbie   Yeah. I think so.
    4   You want me to watch him?
    5   Chad   Yeah.
    6   Debbie   I'd love to. It'd be a pleasure.
    7   Chad   Okay. Thanks. I'll bring him around then.

(Jacobs and Jackson 1983: 299)

As discussed by Elder and Haugh (2018), Chad's utterance in line 2 makes available a potential inference that he wants Debbie to watch his son: an implicature that is calculable on standard Gricean and post-Gricean principles. But at that point – as an implicature – it is only implicitly available. Debbie's response in line 4 makes available her inference that Chad's previous turn may have pertained to a pre-request, as she explicitly makes an offer to watch Chad's son. In this way, it is Debbie's response that puts on record what was previously only implicit from Chad's question, holding Chad accountable for having made available such an inference.

While (16) offers a relatively straightforward way of exposing implicitly communicated messages, as Elder and Haugh (2023) point out, it is possible for recipients to orient to inferences in a myriad of much more subtle ways, without explicitly putting them on record. In (17), we see how a recipient's response can hold a speaker accountable for a given meaning by displaying it as an off record inference, and as such that meaning has the potential to remain 'embedded' in the conversational record (Jefferson 1987, 2003; see also Haugh 2017) if it is not subsequently engaged with.

(17)   (Sirl and Michael, who is staying at Sirl's place, have both stopped outside
         the bathroom at the same time.)
         1   Sirl   What time are you leaving this morning?
         2   Michael   Oh, in about an hour I suppose.
         3   Are you in a hurry to leave?
         4   Sirl   No, no. Just asking.
         5   (2.0)
         6   Michael   Would you like to use the bathroom first?
         7   Sirl   Yeah, sure, if you don't mind.

(Haugh 2007: 94)

In (17), Sirl's turn in line 1 can be seen as a straightforward question about Michael's leaving time, to which Michael responds directly in line 2. But (as discussed by Haugh 2007; Elder and Haugh 2018, 2023; and others) Michael's follow up in line 3, 'Are you in a hurry to leave?' implicitly makes available an inference regarding Sirl's motivations for his prior question, opening up the possibility that Sirl may have made a pre-request to use the bathroom first. Sirl immediately denies being in a hurry, claiming to be 'just asking', and thus taking that interpretation off the table. However, the pause that ensues signals that something is not quite right, leading Michael to ask Sirl directly if he would 'like to use the bathroom first'. Sirl readily agrees.

Elder and Haugh (2023) highlight how Michael appears to expose an inference that Sirl apparently wanted to keep off record. What is of interest here is that Michael's orienting to Sirl wanting to use the bathroom in line 3 is implicit, and hence does not hold Sirl explicitly accountable for having communicated such a message. That is, at this point in the interaction, the relevant message remains embedded in the conversational record, and so Sirl is not obliged to respond to the implicit content of what might be communicated by Michael's inquiry. Nevertheless, Sirl's claim that he was 'just asking' does indicate an awareness that Michael's question was not simply in service of asking about his upcoming plans for the day, and hence evidences his desire to avoid being held accountable for the inference that Michael appears to have drawn. Indeed, the fact that Sirl later accepts the offer to use the bathroom first suggests that it was not the propositional content of Michael's inference in line 3 that was of concern, but the possibility that he might be held accountable for having had any such motivation.

Moving to the most implicit of conversational moves, (18) hints at how *absent* turns can be used to display inferences. Consider the following interaction between Sally (from Australia), and Peter (from the USA), who are meeting for the first time in Australia.

(18) 1 Sally yeah. So why'd you come here?
      2 Peter um (0.5) I was thinking about moving to Australia, just in general.
      3 Sally [oh yeah.]
      4 Peter [cos uh I] like the culture and everything
      5   I've done a few like research projects on it for school
      6   but I was like, I should probably visit there before I decide I just wanna go there.
      7 Sally yeah.
      8 Peter but? yeah. (0.2) still mi:ght. I figure this would b-be a place I'd wanna settle down at.
      9   (0.7)
     10   but I gotta travel a little bit more.
     11 Sally oh yeah.

(CAAT: AmAus02: 1:46, Haugh 2017)

After Sally asks her opening question regarding why Peter decided to go to Australia, he tells her that he's thinking about moving permanently. He offers some reasons for why he likes it there ('I like the culture and everything'), before responding to Sally's original question in line 6 with an account for his current visit, namely that he thought he 'should probably visit' first. He then repeats his motivation in line 8 that he's considering Australia as 'a place I'd wanna settle down at'. At this point, Peter may expect an affiliative response to his disclosure of plans. However, Sally does not respond, resulting in a noticeable pause. The pause itself makes available a potential inference that

Sally is refraining from offering such affiliation, as well as orienting to potential inferences that might have arisen from Peter's previous turn that she is avoiding (such as what opportunities Peter's moving to Australia might open for his relationship with her, see Haugh 2017 on this possibility based on their subsequent interaction). Peter responds by filling the silence and orienting away from the issue of his future move to Australia, instead shifting the topic to his interim plans, namely that he wants to 'travel a little bit more'.

What this example demonstrates is how *absent* turns can provide evidence for the ways in which prior utterances have been understood, and hence can be used to hold speakers accountable for those understandings. It is arguably Sally's lack of response that invited Peter to orient his attention towards what she might have inferred but did not want to put on record, and hence to view those potential inferences as 'unwanted' (see Elder and Haugh 2023 on this point). But of course while silence can be inferentially rich, what has been communicated is usually highly indeterminate. And since an absent turn doesn't communicate anything explicit, it always remains equivocal as to what the speaker may have 'meant' by their not-saying, if indeed they intended to communicate anything at all. This equivocality of potential inferences raises a number of questions for the issue of accountability. Are the inferences that recipients recover through absent turns ones for which the not-saying speaker can be held accountable? And in providing a response to an absent turn, to what extent can a responder hold a previous speaker accountable for something they've inferred through the speaker's not-saying?

3.5 Absent Turns and the Meaning of Silence

Before we tackle those questions, it must be pointed out that silence can – of course – occur for a multitude of reasons, not all of which will be inferential. There are many psychological, emotional and contextual reasons that silence can occur, including not wanting to draw attention to oneself, not being able to find the right words, not knowing how to answer a question, and many others (see Ephratt 2011 for an overview of linguistic and psychological approaches to the study of silence). Some of these types of silence may be involuntary while others may be purposeful. Purposeful – or intentional – silence can include refraining from speaking, for example to encourage a client to keep the floor in a therapy session, or coercing a bartering partner into making the next move in a negotiation. Other non-verbal acts can be inferential in the same way as verbal utterances and, as discussed by Sperber and Wilson (2015), non-verbal acts can vary in determinacy in communicative content just as verbal acts can. For example, while nodding to a question of 'are you attending the talk at 2pm today?' may determinately constitute an answer of 'yes', other non-verbal acts are less clear cut as to their communicative content, if they communicate any at all, such as an appreciative sigh or a shrug of the shoulders. But how far we want to include such communicative moves in the purview of the study of pragmatic inference is up for debate.

The first challenge for the study of the *meaning* of silence is delineating the object of study in the first place. One way of doing this is to look at how the sequential position of silence can affect how that silence is interpreted. Here we consider the concept of 'notably absent turns' (Schegloff 1968; more recently Bilmes 1994): the hearable absence of a second pair part of an adjacency pair which would normally be sequentially due. It is exactly because a silence arises in sequential response positions where it would be expected for talk to occur that it is hearable as absent, that it is presumed to communicate pragmatic inferences. As Schegloff (1968: 1086) says, 'a variety of "strong inferences" can be drawn from the fact of the official absence of an answer, and any member who does not answer does so at the peril of one of those inferences being made'. Such inferences, excepting unavailability from interacting, might include that the non-speaker is giving the cold shoulder, being insulting, or other 'insolent' activities (Schegloff 1968: 1087).

To return to our questions regarding accountability above, Schegloff would have it that an absent response communicates an inference for which the non-speaking participant can be held accountable:

> ... we may say that the conditional relevance of A [answer] on S [summons] entails not only that the nonoccurrence of A is its official absence, but also that that absence is 'accountable'. Furthermore, where an inference is readily available from the absence of an answer, that inference *stands as its account*. (Schegloff 1968: 1087, my emphasis)

While absent turns make available inferences about their absence, looking at recipient responses to absent turns can provide evidence for how those absent turns have been understood. Returning to Peter and Sally in (18) above, in shifting the direction of the interaction, Peter appears to both acknowledge Sally's silence as a response to the potentially awkward inferences that Peter may have opened up in his previous utterance, while also orienting away from them. So, through Peter's response to Sally's absent turn – that signals a lack of encouragement to his possible move to Australia – we see how recipients of silence can orient to the inferences that are made available by others through their silent turns, thereby making available – and in turn holding the other accountable for – their inference of how they have understood that silence.

Now, 'notably absent turns' are most easily observed through a *lack* of talk. We finish this section by looking at how verbal utterances can also function as 'absent turns' by substituting an expected response with an unexpected one. Drew and Hepburn (2016) raise the case of absent apologies. The idea is that not giving an apology implicitly signals that the speaker does not consider an apology to be due, thereby further making available an inference that they do not consider their behaviour to constitute a transgression (see also Heritage et al. 2019).

(19)   (Jessie phones her optician)

1	Desk	Hello Goodwin,
2	Jessie	Um good morning. Er it's Mrs Chandra here, I called in on
3		Thursday to see if I could make an appointment to see Mister
4		Fortis
5		(1.2)
6	Jessie	**And, I haven't heard anything** and I was wondering if, um
7		(Mister Fortis could see me) one day next week.
8		(0.8)
9	Desk	Um I'll just check his diary can you hold a minute (uh [please).
10	Jessie	[Yes, ((9 lines omitted, receptionist asks for caller's name))
[. . .]		
19		(7.0)
20	Fortis	Hello
21	Jessie	Hello?
22	Fortis	**I tried to ring you on Thursday evening but I couldn't get any**
23		**reply**
24	Jessie	Oh dear.
25	Fortis	**It's all right.** Now, when do you want to come in Monday?

(Rahman:1:2:1, adapted from Drew and Hepburn 2016)

In this example, Jessie telephones her optician, explaining in lines 2–6 that she had previously 'called in on Thursday' to make an appointment, but since then 'haven't heard anything'. As Drew and Hepburn (2016) point out, Jessie's account is formulated as a 'complainable matter'. As such, Jessie's account could be heard as considering an apology to be due. However, when the optician (Mr Fortis) comes to the phone, he immediately opens the interaction in lines 22–23 with his own account, stating that 'I tried to ring you on Thursday evening but I couldn't get any reply'. Since Fortis' account contradicts Jessie's prior complaint, it absolves him from having to give an apology, since his prior conduct did not amount to a transgression. Meanwhile, his mentioning that Jessie didn't pick up the telephone can be heard as a shifting of blame from Fortis to Jessie, which could itself be heard as its own complainable matter. Jessie's response, 'Oh dear', however, treats Fortis' account as a misfortune, rather than an action that Jessie is responsible for and that warrants an apology. So, through the hearable absence of non-apology turns in sequential positions where an apology would be both licensed and expected, both Fortis and Jessie make available their respective inferences that no apology is due: inferences for which they can be held accountable.

Now, while Jessie could be held normatively accountable for not having offered an apology where one was hearably licensed, and hence for not considering an apology to be due, Fortis' next turn ('It's all right') responds *as if* an apology had been offered by Jessie. In this way, Fortis explicitly absolves Jessie of her prior conduct, and in so doing, implicitly holds her accountable for having taken responsibility for it, despite Jessie not having actually apologised. Furthermore, Fortis responding as if Jessie had apologised may serve to indicate that it was in her normative duties to have done so, and hence that she *should* assume responsibility for the fact she did not pick up the telephone when Fortis called her.

While recipient responses can serve to demonstrate how a previous speaker's turn has been understood and hence hold the previous speaker accountable for that understanding, the interaction between Jessie and Fortis highlights how disagreements on what has been communicated can lie 'under the surface'. Rather than interactionally achieving a shared meaning of Jessie's non-apology turn, Fortis' response exposes a disagreement between Jessie and Fortis as to who was at fault for their previous lack of communication, and hence how Jessie's non-apology turn has been operationalised. But while Fortis' response may appear to be holding Jessie accountable for having apologised for a previous transgression, it is questionable whether or not Fortis is licensed to do so given Jessie's formulation of her prior turn. This is because normative accountability is not only dependent on recipient uptake, but also on normative meanings (cf. normative commitments, discussed in 3.2), and in this respect, a speaker cannot be held *as* accountable for an aspect of meaning that they can't be seen to have communicated than as for one that is strongly inferable from what they said.

3.6 Combining Approaches to Speaker Meaning, Commitment and Accountability

In this section, we have looked at different approaches to the question of which meanings a speaker could, or should, be held responsible for. Starting with the language system, we can say that speakers are normatively committed to what they say in virtue of the conventions of language use and principles of normative communication. These normative commitments include a wide array of meanings that are derivable from what is said, including entailments, presuppositions and implicatures. As long as a hearer recovers a meaning that falls inside this set of potential inferables, the normative commitment account provides the theoretical rationale for why their inference is possible.

However, while speakers can, in theory, be committed to a vast array of potential messages, the commitments derived from speakers' utterances need not be consciously available to either speakers or hearers. As noted by Ariel (2016), *potential* inferences that are compatible with what the speaker said should not be conflated with speaker *intended* inferences. A cognitive processing account such as Relevance Theory thus provides another dimension to the picture insofar as it can help explain both how hearers come to make the inferences they do, as well as why hearers are *likely* to infer the meanings that they do. As different kinds of meanings are communicated to different degrees of explicitness, a hearer is arguably more strongly licensed to infer that a speaker intended to communicate messages that are explicitly and strongly communicated than those that are indeterminate or weakly communicated. Hence, how committed a speaker is held to particular meanings is a matter of degree, depending on both how explicitly an aspect of meaning has been communicated, as well as how relevant it is to the purposes of the communicative exchange.

The flipside of this coin is that speakers also bear responsibility for the meanings to which they are held committed by hearers. This is because a speaker is presumed to have agency in the way in which they formulate their utterances, and hence they can modulate the extent to which a hearer is likely to hold them committed to what they say. As a hearer is less likely to hold a speaker committed to an implicit meaning than to an explicit one, a speaker can opt to produce their message more or less explicitly, and thereby increase or decrease the degree to which hearers hold speakers committed to the different inferences they communicate (cf. Haugh 2013 on this point). As Hansen and Terkourafi (2023) describe, there are many other sources of information that hearers draw on when making pragmatic inferences that go beyond inferences about speakers' intentions, including conventional meanings of expressions and sequential placement of utterances, but also hearers' assumptions about the activity type, perceived relationship with the speaker, the speaker's identities, and the presence of third parties. That is, hearers' inferences are subject to multiple sources that may have greater or lesser importance in different contexts of utterance.

Now, while hearers can 'hold a speaker committed' by making a *private* inference about what a speaker intended to communicate, hearers can also 'hold a speaker accountable' by making available a *public* inference about what has been communicated through their on record responses. Here the interactional achievement account complements both Relevance Theory as a cognitive processing account and the normative commitment account. We know that participants may hold a range of private inferences regarding what was meant or what was communicated. At the same time, speakers and hearers cannot be expected to entertain all the possible inferences that are normatively licensed by a given utterance. It is through public displays of inferencing which are made available from participants' on record responses that speakers and hearers come to recognise what has been understood and hence which meanings have been interactionally achieved. In turn, the interactional achievement account takes the on record utterances of participants as providing empirical evidence for the inferences that are actually derived and entertained by speakers.

At the same time, just because an aspect of meaning was not subsequently drawn upon does not mean that it was not entertained by participants. Even if a speaker is not publicly held normatively accountable for an aspect of meaning that is not drawn upon by others, they can nevertheless be privately held committed to those meanings by recipients if they happen to entertain them. So, we need both an account of participants' mental states alongside one of publicly available interactional achievements, in order to fully understand the relationship between what is said, meant, and communicated.

It seems that a productive way forward is to take an eclectic approach to the issue of speaker meaning, commitment, and accountability. Admittedly, the different accounts discussed in this section may purport to have disparate aims that make use of different theoretical tools with different starting assumptions, and hence a comparison may seem undue. However, it is exactly by acknowledging points of complementarity between the accounts that they together offer a richer picture of pragmatic inferences and pragmatic inferencing than the accounts in isolation can provide. Such an eclectic approach has been recently adopted by Hansen and Terkourafi (2023) in building their model of hearers' meaning. Here we now focus on how inference itself is viewed intratheoretically to start to build a picture of meaning that targets different aspects of communication and hence that has significant explanatory power.

All in all, we are a step further in understanding why speakers make the inferences they do, and how speakers display those inferences to others. While it is the interactional achievement account that is most amenable to encompassing misunderstandings in its scope of explanation, it has to be remembered that even if meanings are interactionally achieved, it does not mean that speakers always come to shared understandings of what has been communicated. Even though a recipient can hold a speaker normatively accountable for having communicated an off record meaning by making it the object of their future response, displayed inferences can always be disputed by speakers, and when an aspect of meaning is communicated implicitly, a speaker is more strongly licensed to deny that such meanings were 'meant'. Issues of commitment and accountability thus go hand in hand with the issue of how speakers attempt to negotiate their degree of commitment and accountability, leading us to the final topic of this Element: deniability.

4 Inference Strength and Deniability

We have looked at the relationship between the strength of a speaker's intention to communicate a given meaning and the degree to which they can be held committed to that meaning; the relationship between speakers' intentions, formulation of utterances as more or less explicit, and inferences that are licensed from what is said; as well as the relationship between speakers' private mental states and the meanings that speakers are held accountable for by way of being made publicly available on the conversational record. But what about when speakers' and hearers' understandings of what has been communicated diverge beyond the possibility of reconciliation via co-construction: whose meaning is the 'right' meaning?

Well, in truly taking an eclectic approach to the study of pragmatic inference, the 'right' answer to this question will remain somewhat elusive, as it will require deferring to the (theoretical) perspective one takes. We have already suggested that a normative commitment account can help us with the question of what licenses a hearer to make a given inference, the flipside being that a hearer may *not* have the linguistic grounds to make an inference when it lies outside that set of normative commitments. Indeed, as we saw with Fortis and Jessie in (19) in the previous section, such responses are less likely to lead to interactional achievements – in the sense of speakers and hearers agreeing on what has been communicated – when a speaker is held accountable for some aspect of meaning that is not actually derivable from what they said: when it is not a member of the set of *inferable* meanings. At the same time, we have seen how a hearer can make an inference that lies outside this set (e.g. Clark's 'tea' situation, described in (7)), and yet a speaker can accept it if it is not functionally significant, or if it is even beneficial to interactional outcomes (cf. Elder and Beaver 2022), in which case the question of 'whose meaning' is irrelevant when looking for a general description of communication as a joint endeavour.

But, of course it matters to speakers that they are understood in the way that they want to be understood, and when it *is* significant, speakers and hearers can engage in (sometimes heated) debate over what was meant, or what was said. So, perhaps a more pertinent question to ask is: to what extent can a speaker attempt to deny an aspect of meaning that they didn't mean, or, at least, don't want to be held accountable for? The answer to this question has obvious practical repercussions in the management of social relationships all the way to legal disputes that are reliant on what has been said. But it also has theoretical consequences: whether and how speakers are able to deny having said or meant different kinds of meanings offers us insight into the kinds of social and contextual constraints there are on pragmatic inferences.

This section starts with an overview of cancellability of implicatures as a discursive move, considering whether – and if so, under what circumstances – the cancellability of implicatures affords a speaker with 'plausible deniability' for having said, or meant, something that was implicitly communicated. It then moves to consider the interactional effects of denying, demonstrating that it is not only the content of implicatures that can be denied, but also one's commitment to having communicated them (whether or not one intended the recipient to recover them). We finish the section by examining how social aspects of meanings can be negotiated in interaction through a case study on microaggressions, before finishing with some final thoughts on the extent to which a speaker can or should be held committed to unwanted aspects of meaning, can be held accountable for them, and can successfully deny having communicated them.

4.1 Cancellability and Deniability

Implicatures are, by definition and hence in principle, defeasible. This is because implicatures give rise to non-monotonic inferences: they can be 'cancelled' in the face of new, competing information. Grice (1989: 39, 44) identified two types of cancellation: 'explicit cancellation', which involves a speaker adding a subsequent clause to their utterance in order to signal their 'opting out' of a potential inference ('but I don't mean to imply . . . ', 'in fact . . . '), and 'contextual cancellation', which occurs when the context of utterance prevents an inference from arising that could otherwise be inferable from the sentence. For example, in a situation where someone has run out of fuel, uttering (20) to them may implicate that the garage is open and selling fuel; however, adding an explicit cancellation clause 'but it's closed' signals that this putative implicature should not be recovered.

(20)   There is a garage round the corner.

On the other hand, given that one *can* imagine a situation in which (20) might give rise to an implicature that the garage is open and selling fuel, in a situation where it is mutually known that the garage is in fact closed (e.g. because it is out of hours, or it is permanently closed), an utterance of (20) is contextually cancelled: it simply does not arise.

As Jaszczolt (2009, 2023) suggests, it is only explicit cancellation that is empirically observable, while contextual cancellation is only relevant as a thought experiment: an implicature's non-arising is dependent on imagining a situation where it *could* arise, but would not actually arise in a given discourse situation. Explicit cancellation, on the other hand, is a discursive strategy available to speakers when there is a risk of a misunderstanding: when the speaker realises that what they said makes available a potential implicature that is unwanted, they can add a cancellation phrase to signal that the implicature should not be drawn.

Now, while cancellability is typically treated as the archetypal test for implicaturehood, the legitimacy of explicit cancellation as a discursive move is more complex. For example, Jaszczolt (2009) argues that when an implicature acts as the primary meaning of an utterance – i.e. the main message intended by the speaker – its entrenchment in the discourse renders it pragmatically infelicitous to cancel.

Imagine I am in a restaurant, sitting underneath an air conditioning unit and feeling too cold to be comfortable. I get the server's attention and utter (21).

(21)   Excuse me, I'm quite cold under this air conditioning.

I communicate a strong implicature that I would like the air conditioning turned off, to the extent that this implicit meaning constitutes my primary meaning. So it would be very strange for me to add on (21a), for – even if it were true – it would call into question why I bothered the server with the information in (21) in the first place.

(21a)   But I don't mean to say that you should turn it off, I'm quite enjoying the cold.

As Macagno (2023) has argued, theoretical cancellability – retracting unsaid content without logical contradiction – should not be confused with what he calls *practical* cancellability: determining the circumstances under which a cancellation is reasonable and acceptable.

Cancellation as a discursive move can be observed in a variety of ways. Haugh (2013) terms the anticipatory act of cancellation as 'blocking': where a speaker adds a cancellation phrase to block a potential inference from entering the conversational record.[1] However, as he points out, while cancellation is supposed to avoid an implicature from arising, it does so by putting the relevant meaning on record (see also Mandelbaum 2016 on this point). That is, the act of

---

[1] 'Blocking' here should not be confused with the same term used in computational linguistics that describes the phenomenon of restricting (e.g.) morphological word formation or lexical senses due to the existence of competing forms. See e.g. Briscoe et al. (1995) and Embick et al. (in press) for overviews of the latter phenomenon.

cancellation presupposes that there is something to cancel in the first place, but in effect, it ends up putting the unwanted potential implicature on record.

Cases of cancellation via 'blocking' contrast with cases in which a recipient recovers an unwanted inference and explicitly puts it on record. In such cases, Haugh (2013) suggests that cancellation is not really possible in the sense that the implicature is removed from the conversational record. Rather, all speakers can do is modulate their commitment to the implicature through, for example, *denial* (claiming that whatever was inferred by the recipient was not intended by the speaker), *retraction* (claiming that what the recipient inferred was not relevant or applicable to the current discourse), or *clarifying* (claiming what they intended was different to what the recipient inferred). Moreover, he proposes that it is only indeterminate implicatures that are open to interpretation that can be plausibly denied or retracted, but determinate and/or strongly inferable implicatures are less easy to deny, leaving clarification of what was intended as the only interactionally legitimate action, although, as he says, whatever cancellation strategy the speaker employs, it is always open to dispute by hearers. So, even though all implicatures *can* be cancelled by definition, cancellation *as a discursive move* is a gradable property of implicatures.

Pinker et al. (2008) argue that the fact that implicatures afford the speaker 'plausible deniability' provides the motivation to communicate a message implicitly in strategic, adversarial, or at least awkward, situations, such as when attempting sexual come-ons, bribery, or threats: if their communicative attempt backfires, they can always claim they 'didn't mean it that way'. They do admit that when an implicature is highly likely to have been intended by the speaker, the *plausibility* that a speaker's denial is genuine is less likely to be accepted. Nevertheless, drawing on Kahneman and Tversky (1979), who argue that people have a propensity for distinguishing 100 per cent certainty from all other probability values even if they are very high, Pinker et al. maintain that as long as an implicature is *possible* to deny, it is still preferable to adopt an indirect communicative strategy over a direct one when the content to be communicated comes with a risk of adverse consequences.

So while possible deniability may give the speaker a theoretical 'get out' in the face of linguistic adversity, in reality its interactional success is contingent. In line with the literature on commitments, Sternau et al. (2015, 2017) argue that deniability is proportional to explicitness of communication, with explicatures being less deniable than implicatures, and strong implicatures being less deniable than weak implicatures. The latter comparison between strong and weak implicatures has been experimentally corroborated by Bonalumi et al. (2022), reminding us that strategic communication is a much more complex matter than simply whether an aspect of meaning has been explicitly or implicitly communicated, as a strategic speaker also has to navigate how strongly that message is communicated (cf. the discussion in Section 3 on commitment and primary meanings).

Mazzarella (2021) has recently addresses the question of the conditions under which a hearer is likely to accept a speaker's denial. For her, denial involves not only withdrawing the inference in question ('I didn't mean that p'), but also offering an alternative interpretation ('I only meant that q'). By presenting an alternative interpretation, the speaker attempts to modulate the assumptions that the hearer is supposed to employ when interpreting the previous utterance. Building on Camp (2018), who views deniability as a function of the degree of epistemic accessibility of alternative sets of assumptions, Mazzarella develops a taxonomy of ways in which a speaker can attempt to manipulate the context of interpretation: speakers can broaden the context of interpretation by adding on new contextual assumptions; they can exclude some contextual assumptions; or they can reconstruct the context through a combination of adding and excluding contextual assumptions in order for the speaker to arrive at a new interpretation that suits them. To illustrate the latter, she adapts an example from Pinker (2007), reproduced here in (22).

(22)   1   A   Gee, officer, I was wondering whether there might be some way we could take care of the ticket here.
       2   B   You know I can arrest you for a bribe.
       3   A   Oh, I didn't mean it that way, officer. I was just wondering whether we could use a mobile terminal to pay the fine.

In this example, speaker A attempts to both exclude the assumption that 'taking care of the ticket' amounts to a bribery attempt, while adding on a new assumption regarding mobile payment options to reconstruct the context of interpretation of the initial utterance. In other words, the speaker uses *explicit cancellation* by presenting the context of interpretation in which the inference in question should (allegedly) have been *contextually cancelled*.

Mazzarella (2021) uses the framework of Relevance Theory to argue that how plausibly the contextual assumptions can be manipulated, and hence that the denial will be accepted, will depend not only on the accessibility of the new assumptions from the hearer's initial context of interpretation, but also on the cognitive utility of processing the reconstructed context such that it will achieve sufficient cognitive effects. That is, the recipient would expect the speaker's initial utterance to be optimally relevant, hence, the new contextual assumptions should not be radically different from the ones the recipient put the effort into processing in the first place; if the new context would require too much processing effort for too few cognitive effects, it would not be worth the hearer's while, and hence the denial would be unlikely to be accepted.

4.2 Denying Commitment and Avoiding Accountability

In Section 3, we discussed at length how when recipients expose an inference through their responses, they hold the speaker normatively accountable for having communicated it. But of course, sometimes recipients recover and expose meanings that speakers *don't* want to be held accountable for. These can amount to simple misunderstandings when a recipient recovers a message the speaker didn't intend to communicate, which the speaker can choose to deny, correct or clarify. But while speakers can use plausible (or, at least, possible) deniability to their advantage in order to avoid being held accountable for an undesirable inference, denial attempts do not necessarily mean that speakers want to discard the inference altogether. Here we look at cases in which it is not straightforwardly a particular proposition that the speaker wants to remove from the conversational record, but cases where a speaker may be happy for the recipient to entertain, and even act upon, some aspect of meaning, but their denial attempt is to remove their commitment to, and hence avoid being held accountable for, having communicated it.

An attempt to remove the speaker's commitment to an inference, but where that the inference was clearly in line with what the speaker wanted the hearer to infer, can be seen in the following example from the romantic comedy, *Knocked Up* (discussed in Elder 2021).

(23)   (Jack is Alison's boss at a television company; Jill is Jack's assistant. Alison has recently found out she is pregnant. Jack has offered Alison an on-camera role to interview pregnant women, and is meeting with her to discuss the new position.)

1	Jack:	About the work, most immediately, there's going to be some things that you're going to be able to get that other people in the office don't get. One of them: Gym membership.
2	Alison	You want me to . . . lose weight?
3	Jack	(laughing) No I don't want you to lose weight!
4	Jill	(deadpan) No, uh, we can't legally ask you to do that.
5	Jack	We didn't say lose weight.
6	Jill	No.
7	Jack	I might say 'tighten'.
8	Alison	Tight.
9	Jack	A little . . . tighter.
10	Jill	Just like toned and smaller.
11	Jack	Don't make everything smaller. I don't want to generalise that way. Tighter.
12	Jill	We don't want you to lose weight. We just want you to be healthy.
13	Alison	Okay.

14	Jill	You know, by . . . by eating less. We would just like it if you go home and step on a scale, and write down how much you weigh, and subtract it by like twenty.
15	Alison	Twenty.
16	Jill	And then weigh that much.

(*Knocked Up*, 2007, Universal Studios Home Entertainment. Film)

Following Jack's offer of gym membership, Alison immediately seeks to clarify a putative implicature through her clarification question, 'You want me to lose weight?'. Despite this being strongly inferable – given the expected relationship between gym membership, attending the gym, and losing weight – Jack immediately and explicitly denies the putative implicature in his exclamative response, 'No I don't want you to lose weight!'. However, Jill's deadpan contribution, 'we can't legally ask you to do that', casts doubt on Jack's denial attempt, as by providing an account of why they cannot request Alison loses weight, she thereby makes available an inference that in the absence of legal authority they would, in fact, ask her to do so. Jack's further claim that they didn't 'say' lose weight, puts on record that he is renouncing his commitment from that potential inference by making a claim to plausible deniability, yet in making reference to what was said, also strongly implicates that there was something to infer that went beyond what was said. Jack and Jill subsequently work to clarify what the availability of gym membership to Alison might amount to ('tighter'), with Jill reformulating the initial putative implicature in terms of being 'healthy'. Eventually, Jill offers an alternative route that Alison could pursue, namely 'by eating less', further reinforcing the initial 'losing weight' inference, finishing by requesting Alison to subtract 'twenty' from her current weight, 'and then weigh that much'.

In this example, we see Jack and Jill working hard to avoid being put on record as asking Alison to lose weight, despite this being clearly inferable from Jack's initial mentioning of 'gym membership' and Alison holding Jack normatively accountable for it through her clarification question at the start of the interaction. This avoidance is initially attempted through explicit denial, moving to clarification of what else they could have meant, through to finally de facto confirming the inference. So, the more the issue is discussed, the clearer it becomes that Alison's initial inference was both licensed and intended by Jack, and that Jack and Jill's denial attempts were in service of avoiding responsibility for it, rather than avoiding the inference altogether. Moreover, as Elder (2021) notes, it is due to the subsequent negotiation and development of what an inference from mentioning 'gym membership' might mean for Alison that the implicature pertaining to losing weight – that was initially denied – becomes more strongly entrenched and hence less possible to deny, either as a speaker-intended aspect of meaning, or as being committed to having communicated it in the first place.

Such cases are reminiscent of Sperber and Wilson's (1986/1995) delineation of 'mutually manifest' communication. They use the example of Mary who wants Peter to mend her hairdryer but doesn't want to ask him directly. To signal to him her informative intention, she dismantles the hairdryer and leaves the pieces lying around in the hope that he will mend it for her. However, she does not have a communicative intention: she does not want it to be made mutually manifest that she intended him to recover her informative intention. Hence, for Sperber and Wilson, this is not a true instance of 'communication' (see Sperber and Wilson 1986/1995: 30–1; 60–4). In (23), Jack's avoidance of being held accountable for having asked Alison to lose weight could be seen as a case of communicating an informative intention without a communicative intention. But this doesn't seem quite right: Jack ostensibly *did* want Alison to recover the putative implicature; he simply did not want to be put on record as having communicated it.

While deniability of implicatures is typically discussed in terms of explicit attempts to retract a recovered inference, speakers can also suspend inferences in much more subtle ways in order to avoid being held accountable for them. In fact, we have already seen some examples of suspending in our previous discussions, such as Emma's avoiding being held accountable for having asked Betsy to pick her up some food in (11), Sirl avoiding being held accountable for asking to use the bathroom first in (17), and Peter's orienting away from potentially awkward inferences regarding his relationship with Sally in (18). In these examples, the speaker's third position response makes available an inference that something about the recipient's displayed inference did not align with what the speaker wanted to communicate, and hence retroactively works to suspend an inference that has possibly been drawn by the recipient. However, rather than using explicit denial, the inference is suspended implicitly, without putting the inference in question on record.

Recall the interaction between Peter and Sally, repeated below.

(18) 1 Sally yeah. So why'd you come here?
      2 Peter um (0.5) I was thinking about moving to Australia, just in general.
      3 Sally [oh yeah.]
      4 Peter [cos uh I] like the culture and everything

5		I've done a few like research projects on it for school
6		but I was like, I should probably visit there before I decide I just wanna go there.
7	Sally	yeah.
8	Peter	but? yeah. (0.2) still mi:ght. **I figure this would b-be a place I'd wanna settle down at.**
9		**(0.7)**
10		**but I gotta travel a little bit more.**
11	Sally	oh yeah.

(CAAT: AmAus02: 1:46, Haugh 2017)

As we recall from the previous section, Peter responds to Sally's lack of response regarding his future plans to move to Australia by orienting away from this possibility in line 10, expressing that he wants to travel more. While in the previous section we focussed on the possible inferences that could have arisen from Sally's lack of response that results in a hearable pause, here we turn our attention to Peter's attempts to suspend the unwanted inferences (see Elder and Haugh 2023 on unwanted inferences).

What we arguably see from Peter in line 10 is an example of an 'embedded self-correction' (Jefferson 1987, 2003), by which the 'correcting' is achieved implicitly and does not become the primary matter of the interaction. Usually, the object of a correction is clearly observable, even if the correction is itself embedded. A simple example of such an embedded correction is the act of responding to an 'incorrect' pronunciation of a word by responding using the same word with the 'correct' pronunciation. What makes the correction 'embedded' is that the speaker refrains from engaging in meta-level discussion about how to pronounce the word in question, and thus the primary aim of the interaction remains uninterrupted. However, as pointed out by Mandelbaum (2016), embedded self-corrections can be much more subtle and hence difficult to observe, precisely because there is no clear target to which the correction can be tied (see also Jefferson 2003 on this point).

Mandelbaum (2016) devises a practice for observing embedded self-corrections as follows:

(1) Something possibly delicate, problematic, or in some way inapposite is apparently detected by the speaker as it is produced in a turn, or in its immediate aftermath. That is, the turn under way, or just produced, may come to be hearable as performing an action that is in some way delicate, problematic, or inapposite. This possibly inapposite action is not the focal action of the turn, but rather a by-product of some design feature of the way the focal action is implemented.

(2) The speaker adds a unit, often an increment, to the turn, and this unit is apparently designed to remove the possibly available problematic hearing. This addition retroactively adjusts or tweaks the action implemented in the turn it is appended to, detoxifying it without exposing a change, and without making that shift the overt business of talk. (Mandelbaum 2016: 121)

Mandelbaum presents a number of examples in which the speaker apparently notices that what they have just said has a potentially undesirable interpretation, which they self-correct through an immediate adjustment. The case of Peter and Sally is slightly different, insofar as it is not simply Peter noticing he may have communicated something inapposite, but it is arguably Sally's lack of response to Peter's disclosure of settling down in Australia that makes available to Peter that some kind of unwanted inference – such as regarding the possibilities that moving to Australia could open for a potential relationship between Peter and Sally – may have arisen from his previous turn. Moreover, it is possible that Peter's previous utterance *was* designed to give rise to an inference regarding such a potential future relationship. But irrespective of Peter's intentions, or of the way in which he was led to view the inference as unwanted, he nevertheless *did* come to recognise the inference as unwanted, and hence his topic shift in his next turn can be seen as an embedded correction, in turn implicitly suspending the unwanted inference from the conversational record.

What is interesting about such embedded self-corrections is that they simultaneously orient towards an unwanted inference at the same time as diverting attention away. As the participants do not draw on the relevant inferences explicitly, it is unclear which inferences the recipient has recovered, and hence how cognitively accessible they are. In this respect, embedded self-corrections lie somewhere between 'blocking' (anticipatory cancellation) and 'suspending' (retroactive cancellation) (terms from Haugh 2013): it *seems* that something unwanted may have been inferred, but the speaker cannot be sure.

Now, the indeterminacy of the inferences in question may license a denial attempt by the speaker. However, due to the inferences being embedded, any explicit denial would have the undesirable effect of drawing attention to the unwanted inferences. Furthermore, should the speaker attempt to explicitly deny having intended them, a recipient is equally licensed to their own denial of having inferred any such inferences in the first place. The benefit of an embedded self-correction is precisely that it keeps those unwanted inferences off the conversational record and the speaker can avoid being held accountable for them. But note that embedded self-corrections come with their own challenges regarding communicative success: unlike explicit denial, the inferences in question are not completely 'off the table', but they are merely 'parked' through the act of diverting the attention away.

4.3 Denying as Socially (In)appropriate: A Case Study on Microaggressions

We finish this section by drawing attention to one further factor that can affect the deniability of inferences. As Mazzarella (2021) describes, how likely a denial is to be accepted by a recipient depends on how cognitively accessible the new, reframed context of interpretation of the initial utterance – as proposed from the denial attempt – is from the original context of interpretation, and how great the cognitive effects will be from processing the new context. Here we turn our attention to cases in which even if a speaker's denial of their *intention* is accepted, what can matter to recipients is whether a denial attempt is a socially appropriate move to make in the first place. We do this through the lens of microaggressions: communicative acts that denigrate an individual or group by referencing some aspect of their social identity.

Before we get into the question of the deniability of microaggressions, there are some key identification challenges to address first. As McClure and Rini (2020) point out, what counts as a microaggression is not uniformly agreed in the scholarly literature. Accounts differ in their focus: some examine the motivations of the perpetrator, others the feelings of the receiver, and others more broadly focus on the unconscious societal biases that they reveal. Unsurprisingly, the perspective one adopts has repercussions for what will 'count' as a microaggression.

What *is* generally agreed is that microaggressions differ from blatantly and intentionally offensive acts in that they are covertly communicated and stem from underlying prejudices. So, what makes them relevant to our discussion here is that, since they are typically covertly communicated, they arm the perpetrator with plausible deniability that they intended to communicate an offensive message (Jones 2016). But there is a further complication in that microaggressions can differ in their degree of *intended* offensiveness, in turn rendering them difficult to identify, both theoretically and by recipients themselves (Elder 2021). Covertly communicated, intentionally offensive 'micro-assaults' (Sue 2010) – from which the microaggressive content is intended to be recoverable by the recipient – lay the strongest claim to implicaturehood: they are speaker intended, implicitly communicated, and yet defeasible. On the other hand, unintentionally offensive 'microinsults' (Sue 2010) are not strictly implicatures as they are not speaker intended; however, as we will see below, this does not render them immune from causing offence.

The following case study highlights the complexities of these issues. *RuPaul's Drag Race* is an American reality competition television series in which contestants engage in a series of challenges in a bid to win the title of 'America's Next Superstar Drag Queen' (Hughes 2008). In December 2020, the contestants for the show's upcoming Season 13 were revealed via livestream by the programme's official YouTube channel (RuPaul's Drag Race 2020). Following this pre-season premiere, one of the contestants, Elliott with 2 Ts, was invited to appear on the YouTube channel of Alexis Mateo (a previous contestant of the show) to discuss the new cast of contestants and their runway outfits along with two other drag queens, Coco Montrese and Kahanna Montrese (also both previous contestants). In this extract, the four drag queens are discussing one of the new contestants for the upcoming season, Symone, a black drag queen.

(24)	1	Kahanna	I feel like, when, okay↓(.) It's very evident whe::n a black girl is pushed (mimics pushing someone with her hands) to play↑ [the black girl↑]
	2	Alexis	[Yeah]
	3	Kahanna	She:: just gave me(.) ['this is me.] This is <u>me</u>'.
	4	Coco	[It's natural]
			(Elliott lifts index finger to speak, everyone falls silent)
	5	Elliott	**She (.) is (.) in a word, black girl magic↓**
	6	Kahanna	[Yeah]
	7	Coco	[Right]
			(All nod in approval)
	8	Elliott	That is, that is what she brought↑ she felt (.) that (.) <u>that</u> should be her message
	9	Alexis	[Right]
	10	Kahanna	[Mm]
			(All nod in approval)
	11	Elliott	**and it was (.) she (.) [but she did it so <u>elegantly</u> though↓]**
	12	Alexis	[and she looked <u>ama::zing</u>]
	13	Coco	Yes↓
	14	Elliott	**it wasn't [aggressive↓ It wasn't <u>aggressive</u> (.) It was done (.)]**
	15	Kahanna	[Mmm (nodding) You can't come for it. It was so::: put together]
	16	Elliott	**[it was done] [with taste↓]**
	17	Alexis	[Yes↓ So::: gorgeous]
	18	Coco	[You could tell]
	19	Elliott	**[Done with taste, yeah↓] (nodding)**
	20	Coco	[You could tell.] Her personality was just [:::] flawless.
	21	Elliott	[Definitely]

(MissAlexisMateo 2021, from 00:17:50)

During the interview, the other drag queens displayed agreement with Elliott's assessment of Symone, and its airing on YouTube did not receive negative feedback at the time of posting. However, in January 2021 after the first few episodes of the new season had aired, the interview later resurfaced when a Twitter user commented on Elliott's language choice, reproduced in (25).[2]

(25)   not to be messy on main but something about elliott saying symone is 'black girl magic without being aggressive' makes me very uncomfortable

This tweet sparked various responses, indicating a range of attitudes towards the content of Elliott's assessment of Symone, as well as Elliott's perceived attitude towards Symone, or people of colour more broadly. For example, some users questioned the rationale behind Elliott's comment, such as in (26) and (27), charging Elliott with holding negative expectations regarding Symone's demeanour.

(26)   was she expecting symone to be aggressive i-

(27)   'without being aggressive' is so backhanded . . . like she was surprised symone was so elegant

The descriptions in these comments are arguably licensed through the explicit content of the relevant utterances that Elliott produced in the initial interview reproduced in (24). The use of sentence-initial 'but' in line 11, 'but she did it so elegantly though', immediately indicates that an implicit contrast was being drawn. Indeed, this contrast is bolstered by putting emphasis on the word 'elegantly', putting that lexical item into focus, and hence giving rise to the presupposition that it belongs to some set of salient alternatives. The availability of a contrast is then given extra strength by the use of sentence-final 'though'. Now, while at this point the object of contrast is still implicit, the utterance gives rise to a licensed inference that it was in some way surprising that Symone's runway look was executed 'elegantly'. The implicit contrast is immediately made explicit in her next turn in line 14, when she utters 'it wasn't aggressive. It wasn't aggressive!', thus putting on record the

---

[2] In line with standard practice, while the names of public figures have been retained, the usernames of ordinary Twitter users have been redacted (Townsend and Wallace 2016), and only the textual material from the relevant tweets has been reproduced. While tweets are traceable via the examples presented here, their being published on Twitter as an open, publicly available searchable online platform licenses their use in academic research, as per guidance on internet research ethics (franzke et al. 2020). Moreover, their inclusion in the discussion is not to cast judgement on the attitudes presented, but merely to discuss the metapragmatic insights they offer to scholarly debates on the role of speaker intentions, deniability, commitment, and accountability.

object of contrast (i.e. elegant versus aggressive), and hence licensing an inference (whether intended or not) that she had an expectation that Symone's look could have been 'aggressive'.

That this conclusion is strongly inferable may underlie the rationale for another Twitter user's response in (28), that refutes the status of Elliott's comments as microaggressive in exchange for 'literally calling black women aggressive'.

(28)   This isn't even a micro aggression she is literally calling black women aggressive, no wonder she was eliminated twice

Of course, it has to be recognised that the word 'literally' is colloquially used in figurative contexts, and may have been done so by this Twitter user. Nevertheless, juxtaposing the 'literal' with a microaggression supports our above assumption that microaggressions are implicitly communicated, at the same time suggesting that since to describe black women as 'aggressive' is so culturally ingrained, it is akin to literal meaning. In other words, the licensed inference pertaining to an expectation of Symone's aggression due to availability of contrasts as described above, extends to an inference pertaining to assumptions about black women in general due to its occurrence in this socionormative context, that is, the context of a white person ascribing attributes to a black person.

Other users confirmed this broader inference as licensed thereby recognising the import that her words had in this social context, while at the same time taking the stance that Elliott didn't realise the connotations behind what she'd said (29), that she didn't intend to be offensive ('it didn't come from a bad place') (30), and that they hope she is able to learn how her language use was problematic (30) and (31).

(29)   Oh lord. She has just no idea how messed up that is

(30)   Instead of dragging her y'all could just let her know what was wrong ... it didn't come from a bad place.

(31)   Damn ... Elliot is really growing on me but idk how to feel about this. I hope she can find the recourses to see what she said is problematic.

All in all, the online reaction to Elliott's description of Symone points towards the general conclusions that Elliott committed a transgression through her choice of words. Furthermore, through these comments, the Twitter users attempted to hold Elliott accountable for having communicated a negatively charged message, but did not uniformly hold her committed to having intended to communicate it.

On the same day that the initial video resurfaced online, Elliott posted a message on Twitter, stating:

(32)   My intentions were never to refer to anyone's message as being 'aggressive'. I was describing her drag, but the words should have used were 'runway ready to wear', 'not over the top', 'understated in a high fashion way'. The word aggressive was never meant to reflect her personality or her message, and admittedly I mis-used the term black girl magic to describe her aesthetic, and have been made aware that this term isn't a blanket statement for the appreciation of blackness but inherently social in nature. (Elliott with 2 Ts 2021)

In this statement, we can see Elliott engaging in a range of cancellation actions, denying that she intended to describe Symone's message or personality as 'aggressive', instead clarifying that she had used the term 'aggressive' to describe Symone's drag, while admitting that there were more appropriate descriptions she could have used and thereby implicitly – but note not explicitly – retracting her use of the word. She admits that her use of the term 'black girl magic' was inappropriate, although this was not seemingly the phrase that was at issue.

The comments that Elliott's message received on Twitter ranged in the degree to which they accepted the message as an apology. On the one hand, some comments acknowledged the mismatch between Elliott's words and their conventional meanings in this context and her intended message, as in (33).

(33)   We love you Elliot, we are all learning and sometimes do word things differently than we intend to x

Others similarly acknowledged Elliott's lack of intention to offend, but were more concerned with the recipients' feelings as a result of Elliott's words, irrespective of those intentions.

(34)   It's okay to explain your intentions but what actually matters is the perception and the fact that your actions hurt people. No matter what or how you meant it.

This type of response indicates that what can matter to people goes beyond the speaker's intentions; even if a recipient accepts that the speaker didn't mean to communicate what they did, they may still want the speaker to bear responsibility for it. This is demonstrated more strongly in (35), where the author takes issue with whether Elliott's message constituted an apology, and hence whether she admitted she had committed a wrongdoing.

(35)   You didn't even say the word sorry or I apologise, nor did you acknowledge who the micro aggressions were against (Symone and the Chicago girls). This is an explanation, not an apology

As the author of (35) states, Elliott's message does not directly address Symone or others who the offending message targeted (or was perceived to have targeted), nor did she explicitly present the message as an apology.

After the season of *RuPaul's Drag Race* ended in April 2021, Symone was interviewed on EW's *Binge* podcast, in which she was asked about her feelings on Elliott's microaggressions. An extract from her response is reproduced in (36).

(36) 1 Symone it <u>is</u> in a way offensive↑ because (1.5) my art is my art and it sh – and it shouldn't matter if it wa – if it was aggressive the entire time like none of that matters

2 it was .hh (.) my art and for you to <u>say</u> that, that type of mindset, those – those types of words, those type of microaggressions .hh, are literally what <u>leads</u> (.) to what happened this summer with (.) um (2) George Floyd.

3 So (.) my feelings are – (.) at first, I wasn't – (.) I wasn't taken aback, because I was like 'oh, maybe she misspoke'

4 but then what <u>really</u> got me (.) was her going online and <u>defend</u>ing it, saying sh::::e was complimenting me

5 and people were const – were (.) trying to explain to her what was going on, she still (.) didn't want to hear it or to receive it↓ so at that point it's kind of like I'm done↑

(EW's *Binge* 2021, from 00:27:35)

Here we see Symone reporting that she was initially forgiving towards Elliott, keeping open the possibility that 'she misspoke' (line 3), and hence not holding her committed to having intended any offence towards Symone through her words. However as we see, it was Elliott's subsequent response that led Symone to find the incident offensive, as in line 4 she takes issue with Elliott's attempts to defend herself by reframing her meaning from an offensive message to a complimenting one. That is, while Elliott may not have had an offensive intention at the time of utterance, her denial attempts were seen to focus too strongly on clarifying her intentions, rather than accepting responsibility for having communicated an offensive message, irrespective of her awareness of having done so. Indeed, later in the interview following this extract, Symone describes the 'apology' message as 'performative', noting how Elliott had failed to take accountability for what she said.

To summarise, we can observe that Elliott's initial utterances in (24) referred to Symone's drag, bolstering her later claim in (32) that she didn't intend to refer to anyone's message as 'aggressive'. Indeed, we can observe that Elliott in fact stated the opposite, namely that Symone *wasn't* aggressive. However, in using the term 'aggressive', she made available an inference regarding the possibility that Symone *could* have been aggressive, and by juxtaposing it with the apparent compliment that she was 'elegant', further made available the inference that being aggressive is an undesirable attribute to have displayed. So, even if Elliott didn't intend any offence by her statements, there remains the sociopragmatic question of why Elliott formulated her opinion in this way in the first place. A possible response to this question is that the formulation of her intended compliment was due to her unconscious association between the term 'aggressive' and black women more generally, thus classifying it as a microaggression.

The online response to both her use of the term and her subsequent apology message on Twitter demonstrate how the microaggressive meaning was perceived as unintended, but nevertheless offensive due to its meaning in this socionormative context and the associations it reinforces in society. Indeed, as we see from Symone's response in (36), any outstanding issues were not with Elliott's intentions regarding whether she was describing Symone as aggressive or not; as Symone outlines in line 1 above, even if Symone's art *was* aggressive (and hence if Elliott had described her as such), it was the use of the word 'aggressive' without attributing or acknowledging its microaggressive potential that remains problematic. So, the backlash against Elliott's response was not wholly due to her lack of awareness of this meaning, and hence her degree of intended offence, but due to her unwillingness to engage with the fact that her choice of words had these connotations, and the societal biases that they reveal and sustain.

4.4 Deniability as a Lens Onto 'What Is Meant' and 'What Is Communicated'

By considering the issue of deniability, we have come full circle back to the issues of commitment and accountability, illustrating the interplay between speakers' intentions, recipients' responses, and the negotiation of meaning.

First, while implicatures are in principle cancellable and licence the speaker plausible deniability, the success of both cancellation and denial of implicatures depends on a number of factors. These include: how strongly the relevant meaning is intended to be communicated; how explicitly the relevant meaning is communicated; how explicitly the relevant meaning is exposed by the recipient; and how plausible a revised context of interpretation is such that the hearer will accept the denial. That is, neither cancellation nor denial as discursive strategies are automatic by-products of implicatures, but are contingent on their linguistic, cognitive, and contextual environments.

Next, cancellation and denial are typically studied in terms of the propositions that they avoid; however, we have also seen that speakers can avoid being held accountable for having communicated something, even when they might welcome the recipient (privately) recovering the propositional content of that message. How such avoidance is achieved can also range from explicit ('I didn't say that!') to implicit, where the correction is itself embedded in the conversational record.

Finally, we have seen how speakers' intentions should not always be given primacy in determining what has been communicated, either in terms of the inferences that are made available and hence licensed by speakers' utterances, or in terms of the inferences that are actually made by recipients. In our case study on microaggressions, we have seen that even if a speaker can legitimately deny an offensive intention, even claiming to have intended to offer a compliment, what can matter to recipients is how the speaker *accepts responsibility* for having committed a linguistic transgression.

Calling a speaker out for their choice of words holds the speaker normatively accountable for having communicated the messages that are normatively available from what was said. But note that in doing so, a recipient does not necessarily expect the speaker to admit their *intentions* for having communicated an offensive message. Recall from the end of Section 3 the difference between publicly holding a speaker accountable for a message and privately holding a speaker committed to having intended it. The *RuPaul's* example demonstrates more clearly how these are separate actions: publicly holding a speaker accountable for having communicated a message does *not* presuppose that the recipient considers the speaker to have intended it, and therefore does not amount to holding the speaker committed to that message. In other words, a recipient can hold the speaker accountable for having communicated a message, even in the absence of the speaker's intention to do so. In this respect, it is possible for speakers to agree on 'what was meant' – or not meant, in this case – while disagreeing on 'what was communicated'.

5 Concluding Remarks on the Study of Pragmatic Inference

Speakers can communicate much more than the words they utter. They can communicate implicit meanings that they intend the hearer to recognise and recover, or they can inadvertently communicate meanings through their words without realising they've done so. Recipients can privately entertain the meanings they think the speaker wanted to communicate, and they can also recover other meanings that are available from the speaker's words whether or not they think the speaker meant them. Recipients can display the meanings they've recovered through the way they respond to speakers, and participants can all work to publicly co-construct meanings together.

This Element has promoted the view that all of these interactional phenomena should be captured and explained in the study of pragmatic inference. Three theoretical accounts – the cognitive, the normative, and the interactional achievement accounts – have been outlined here, each with their own theoretical agenda, their own assumptions regarding the input to description and explanation, and thus their own conclusions about the nature of pragmatic inference. Individually, they can account for some of the phenomena described above. But – their differences notwithstanding – together, they offer a far richer picture of meaning in communication that can at least make a start on accounting for them all.

A running theme throughout our discussions has been the questioning of the role of speakers' intentions in a theory of communication that has both descriptive and explanatory power. A strong motivation for retaining intentions as a theoretical tool is exactly that people inevitably have feelings about what they have or have not intended to communicate, and recipients can form beliefs about the mental states of their interlocutors, and these are feelings that are worth prioritising when aiming for a theory of communication that reflects cognitive reality. At the same time, speaker intentions are not the be all and end all: as we have seen, disputes over meanings may leave intentions by the wayside, focussing on socionormative meanings and attributions of responsibility. Speaker intentions will not always be the trump that settles all communicative conflict; we not only want to account for what people think, but also what they do and why they do it.

All three of the accounts considered here depart, in one way or another, from the idea that a speaker's intention is determinate of the meanings the speaker communicates. While Relevance Theory maintains speaker intentions in its explanatory toolbox, it does so from the hearer's perspective, and to this end allows that hearers can recover meanings that were intended by the speaker to different degrees. As such, speakers can be held committed to meanings to different extents, depending on how strongly the speaker is held to have intended to communicate them. The normative account – as propounded by Geurts (2019) among others – is not concerned with speaker intentions at all, insofar as it considers principles of rationality to explain the inferences that are licensed by a given utterance. And the interactional achievement account stemming from Conversation Analysis relatedly relies on speakers' agency in displaying understandings, making available inferences as they would be expected to arise in a given sequential context.

While Grice's early work is often cited as the foundation for the intentional view of pragmatic inference, we can find elements of all three of these accounts in Grice's writing, as he appealed to expectations about meaning$_{NN}$:

> Explicitly formulated linguistic (or quasilinguistic) intentions are no doubt comparatively rare. In their absence we would seem to rely on very much the same kinds of criteria as we do in the case of non-linguistic intentions where there is a general usage. An utterer is *held to intend to convey* what is normally conveyed (or normally intended to be conveyed), and we require a good reason for accepting that a particular use diverges from the general usage (e.g. he never knew or had forgotten the general usage). (Grice 1989: 222, my emphasis)

At the same time, in taking this kind of eclectic approach to the study of meaning, we do inevitably depart from Grice regarding the object of study, as pragmatic inference is no longer simply the recovery of Gricean implicatures. As we know, implicatures can be strongly or weakly communicated and they can range from determinate to indeterminate. And even further than this, we have gone so far as to suggest that absent turns that don't *say* anything at all can also make available inferences.

Admittedly, when we go that far into pragmatic inferencing – including inferences that are available from absent turns or even silences – we run the risk of developing a 'theory about everything', through which anything can be inferred from anything. And while of course we *can* make inferences from non-linguistic acts, it remains a point of contention how far it is feasible that we can systematically account for them in a theory of communication with any explanatory and/or predictive power, or even how desirable it is to do so in a theory of *linguistic* communication that takes linguistic acts as its input. Scholars like Stanley (2000: 396) have warned that contextual input is necessarily unconstrained when interpreting 'kicks under the table and taps on the shoulder' and hence require a different set of tools to handle them than the kind needed for semantic interpretation of what is said. But it is only a stone's throw away from current contextualist orientations that allow for free enrichment (e.g. Relevance Theory, Recanati) or overriding (e.g. Default Semantics) of linguistic forms in obtaining the main message communicated to use those same contextualist tools to explain how context combines with the practice of not-saying to give rise to different kinds of inferences. In taking an eclectic approach to the kinds of inputs, observations, and principles that inform our account, such an account is not only feasible, but it is necessary if we are to offer a theory of communication that truly reflects how people use, understand and co-construct natural language.

While on the one hand we can question what the input to pragmatic inferencing ought to look like, on the other we can also consider what form we expect the resulting inferences to take. In the spirit of post-Gricean contextualism, we might be tempted to limit ourselves to inferences qua propositions: aspects of meaning that can be represented in terms of their truth conditions. We have tacitly followed this limitation in this Element, focussing in the main on representational aspects of meaning that can be recovered from what is said. And indeed, once we start considering inferences that extend beyond the representational content of what is communicated, we enter a minefield that can easily proliferate. But just because the path is very tangled, does not mean we should not attempt to cross it. We just have to be prepared to take on the challenge of how to study this vast array of inferences – the subplicit inferences that 'glide into the mind of the hearer as side effects of what is said or not said' (Bertuccelli Papi 2000: 147) – with systematicity and explanatory power.

To finish, it is hopefully clear that the way in which pragmatic inference is conceptualised and operationalised is not only relevant to linguistic theory. Issues of what is said, meant and communicated are of tantamount importance in any arena of society where communication is of primary importance, which impacts debates in ethics, law, and sociology, as well as any domain in which linguistic conflict may arise. Unresolved misunderstandings can have serious negative and lasting outcomes on interpersonal relationships, and these can be further fuelled when people's perceptions of social factors are held responsible for communicative conflict, such as when racial, ethnic, gender or religious differences are at issue. The (mis)attribution of speaker intentions can have real-life ramifications for the ways in which people handle misfired jokes that inadvertently cause offence, on the extent to which a speaker can legitimately 'take back' something that was said but not meant, all the way to dealing with microaggressions that negatively target some aspect of a person's social characteristics, whether intentionally or not. This Element has offered a handful of perspectives that together highlight the issues at stake when distinguishing different types of pragmatic inference and how they function in interaction, in turn furthering our understanding of interactional processes of meaning negotiation that are of paramount importance for real-life communication conflict resolution.

References

Ariel, Mira. 2002. Privileged interactional interpretations. *Journal of Pragmatics* 34(8): 1003–44. https://doi.org/10.1016/S0378-2166(01)00061-3.

Ariel, Mira. 2016. Revisiting the typology of pragmatic interpretations. *Intercultural Pragmatics* 13(1): 1–35. https://doi.org/10.1515/ip-2016-0001.

Arundale, Robert B. 1999. An alternative model and ideology of communication for an alternative to politeness theory. *Pragmatics* 9: 119–53. https://doi.org/10.1075/prag.9.1.07aru.

Arundale, Robert B. 2008. Against (Gricean) intentions at the heart of human interaction. *Intercultural Pragmatics* 5(2): 229–58. https://doi.org/10.1515/IP.2008.012.

Arundale, Robert B. 2013. Conceptualizing 'interaction' in interpersonal pragmatics: Implications for understanding and research. *Journal of Pragmatics* 58: 12–26. https://doi.org/10.1016/j.pragma.2013.02.009.

Arundale, Robert B. 2020. *Communicating & Relating: Constituting Face in Everyday Interacting*. Oxford: Oxford University Press.

Bach, Kent 1994. Semantic slack: What is said and more. In: Savas L. Tsohatzidis (ed). *Foundations of Speech Act Theory: Philosophical and Linguistic Perspectives*. London: Routledge, pp. 267–291.

Beaver, David I., Bart Geurts and Kristie Denlinger. 2021. Presupposition. In: Edward N. Zalta (ed). *The Stanford Encyclopedia of Philosophy* (Spring 2021 ed.). https://plato.stanford.edu/archives/spr2021/entries/presupposition/.

Bertuccelli-Papi, Marcella. 2000. *Implicitness in Text and Discourse*. Pisa: Edizoni ETS.

Bianchi, Claudia. 2021. Discursive injustice: The role of uptake. *Topoi* 40: 181–90. https://doi.org/10.1007/s11245-020-09699-x.

Bilmes, Jack. 1994. Constituting silence: Life in the world of total meaning. *Semiotica* 98(1–2): 73–87. https://doi.org/10.1515/semi-1994-981-204.

Bonalumi, Francesca, Johannes Mahr, Pauline Marie and Nausicaa Pouscoulous. 2022. Beyond the implicit/explicit dichotomy: The pragmatics of commitment, accountability, and plausible deniability. *PsyArXiv* [Preprint]. https://doi.org/10.31234/osf.io/z2bqt.

Bonalumi, Francesca, Thom Scott-Phillips, Julius Tacha and Christophe Heintz. 2020. Commitment and communication: Are we committed to what we mean, or what we say? *Language and Cognition* 12(2): 1–25. https://doi.org/10.1017/langcog.2020.2.

Boulat, Kira. 2015. Hearer-oriented processes of strength assignment: A pragmatic model of commitment. *Belgian Journal of Linguistics* 29: 19–40. https://doi.org/10.1075/bjl.29.01bou.

Brandom, Robert B. 1994. *Making It Explicit: Reasoning, Representing and Discursive Commitment*. Cambridge, MA: Harvard University Press.

Briscoe, Ted, Copestake Ann and Lascarides Alex. 1995 Blocking. In: Patrick Saint-Didzier and Evelyne Viegas (eds). *Computational Lexical Semantics*. Cambridge: Cambridge University Press, pp. 273–302.

Brown, Penelope and Stephen C. Levinson. 1987. *Politeness: Some Universals in Language Usage*. Cambridge: Cambridge University Press.

Camp, Elisabeth. 2018. Insinuation, common ground. In: Daniel Fogal, Daniel W. Harris and Matt Moss. *New Work on Speech Acts*. New York: Oxford University Press, pp. 40–65.

Carson Thomas L. 2010. *Lying and Deception: Theory and Practice*. Oxford: Oxford University Press.

Carston, Robyn. 1988. Implicature, explicature, and truth-theoretic semantics. In: Ruth M. Kempson (ed). *Mental Representations: The Interface between Language and Reality*. Cambridge: Cambridge University Press, pp. 155–81.

Carston, Robyn. 2002. *Thoughts and Utterances: The Pragmatics of Explicit Communication*. Oxford: Blackwell.

Clark, Herbert H. 1996. *Using Language*. Cambridge: Cambridge University Press.

Clark, Herbert H. 1997. Dogmas of understanding. *Discourse Processes* 23(3): 567–98. https://doi.org/10.1080/01638539709545003.

Drew, Paul and Alexa Hepburn. 2016. Absent apologies. *Discourse Processes* 53(1–2): 114–31. https://doi.org/10.1080/0163853X.2015.1056690.

Dynel, Marta. 2016. With or without intentions: Accountability and (un)intentional humour in film talk. *Journal of Pragmatics* 95: 67–98. https://doi.org/10.1016/j.pragma.2015.11.010.

Elder, Chi-Hé. 2019. Negotiating what is said in the face of miscommunication. In: Piotr Stalmaszczyk (ed). *Philosophical Insights into Pragmatics*. Berlin: Walter de Gruyter, pp. 107–26.

Elder, Chi-Hé. 2021. Microaggression or misunderstanding? Implicatures, inferences and accountability. *Journal of Pragmatics* 179: 37–43. https://doi.org/10.1016/j.pragma.2021.04.020.

Elder, Chi-Hé and David Beaver. 2022. 'We're running out of fuel': When does miscommunication go unrepaired? *Intercultural Pragmatics* 19(5): 541–70. https://doi.org/10.1515/ip-2022-5001.

Elder, Chi-Hé and Eleni Savva. 2018. Incomplete conditionals and the syntax-pragmatics interface. *Journal of Pragmatics* 138: 45–59. https://doi.org/10.1016/j.pragma.2018.09.015.

Elder, Chi-Hé and Kasia M. Jaszczolt. Forthcoming. Towards a flexible functional proposition for dynamic discourse meaning. In: Hiroaki Tanaka, Kaori Hata, Etsuko Yoshida and Masataka Yamaguchi (eds). *Towards a Dynamic Pragmatics*, volume 4. Tokyo: Kaitakusha.

Elder, Chi-Hé and Michael Haugh. 2023. Exposing and avoiding unwanted inferences in conversational interaction. *Journal of Pragmatics*. 218: 115–32. https://doi.org/10.1016/j.pragma.2023.09.014.

Elder, Chi-Hé and Michael Haugh. 2018. The interactional achievement of speaker meaning: Towards a formal account of conversational inference. *Intercultural Pragmatics* 15(5): 593–625. https://doi.org/10.1515/ip-2018-0021.

Elliott with 2 Ts [@theelliottqueen]. 2021. Twitter, 21 January 2021. https://twitter.com/theelliottqueen/status/1352388093404303360?s=20&t=U8i7IU9yE_zfJubFsJW-8w [Accessed 7 March 2022].

Embick, David, Johanna Benz and Lefteris Paparounas. 2023. Blocking effects. In: Peter Ackema, Sabrina Bendjaballah, Eulàlia Bonet, and Antonio Fábregas (eds). *The Wiley Blackwell Companion to Morphology*. Hoboken, NJ: Wiley-Blackwell. https://doi.org/10.1002/9781119693604.morphcom010

Ephratt, Michal. 2011. Linguistic, paralinguistic and extralinguistic speech and silence. *Journal of Pragmatics* 43(9): 2286–307. https://doi.org/10.1016/j.pragma.2011.03.006.

EW's Binge. 2021. RuPaul's Drag Race season 13. Podcast episode, April. https://open.spotify.com/episode/1OtJeoElx4zCjefR70Znz9?si=ZfnOKvd4Q5axT-s-q7A4DA&nd=1 [Accessed 7 March 2022].

franzke, aline shakti, Anja Bechmann, Michael Zimmer, Charles M. Ess. 2020. Internet Research: Ethical Guidelines 3.0. *The Association of Internet Researchers*. https://aoir.org/reports/ethics3.pdf

Geurts, Bart. 2019. Communication as commitment sharing: Speech acts, implicatures, common ground. *Theoretical Linguistics* 45(1–2): 1–30. https://doi.org/10.1515/tl-2019-0001.

Gregoromichelaki, Eleni, Ruth Kempson, Matt Purver et al. 2011. Incrementality and intention-recognition in utterance processing. *Dialogue and Discourse* 2(1): 199–233. https://doi.org/10.5087/dad.2011.109.

Grice Paul. 1957. Meaning. *The Philosophical Review* 66 (3): 377–388. Reprinted in Grice, 1989, pp. 213–23.

Grice, Paul. 1975. Logic and conversation. In: Peter Cole and Jerry L. Morgan (eds). *Syntax and Semantics 3*. New York: Academic Press, pp. 41–58. Reprinted in Grice, 1989, pp. 22–40.

Grice, Paul. 1978. Further notes on logic and conversation. In: Peter Cole and Morgan Jerry L. (eds). *Syntax and Semantics 9*. New York: Academic Press, pp. 113–27. Reprinted in Grice, 1989, pp. 41–57.

Grice, Paul. 1989. *Studies in the Way of Words*. Cambridge, MA: Harvard University Press.

Hamblin, Charles Leonard. 1970. *Fallacies*. London: Methuen.

Hansen, Maj-Britt Mosegaard and Marina Terkourafi. 2023. We need to talk about Hearer's meaning! *Journal of Pragmatics* 208: 99–114. https://doi.org/10.1016/j.pragma.2023.02.015.

Harris, Daniel W. 2019. Intention and commitment in speech acts. *Theoretical Linguistics* 45(1–2): 53–67. https://doi.org/10.1515/tl-2019-0004.

Haugh, Michael. 2007. The co-constitution of politeness implicature in conversation. *Journal of Pragmatics* 39(1): 84–110. https://doi.org/10.1016/j.pragma.2006.07.004.

Haugh, Michael. 2008. The place of intention in the interactional achievement of implicature. In: Istvan Kecskes and Jacob L. Mey (eds). *Intention, Common Ground and the Egocentric Speaker-Hearer*. Berlin: Mouton de Gruyter, pp. 45–85.

Haugh, Michael. 2011. Practices and defaults in interpreting disjunction. In: Kasia M. Jaszczolt and Keith Allan (eds). *Salience and Defaults in Utterance Processing*. Berlin: Mouton de Gruyter, pp. 189–226. https://doi.org/10.1515/9783110270679.189.

Haugh, Michael. 2013. Implicature, inference and cancellability. In: Alessandro Capone, Franco Lo Piparo and Marco Carapezza (eds). *Perspectives on Pragmatics and Philosophy*. New York: Springer, pp. 133–151. https://doi.org/10.1007/978-3-319-01011-3_6.

Haugh, Michael. 2017. Prompting offers of assistance in interactions. *Pragmatics and Society* 8(2): 183–207. https://doi.org/10.1075/ps.8.2.02hau.

Heritage, John. 1984. *Garfinkel and Ethnomethodology*. Cambridge: Polity Press.

Heritage, John, Chase Wesley Raymond and Paul Drew. 2019. Constructing apologies: Reflexive relationships between apologies and offenses. *Journal of Pragmatics* 142: 185–200. https://doi.org/10.1016/j.pragma.2019.01.001.

Horn, Laurence R. 2004. Implicature. In: Laurence R. Horn and Gregory Ward (eds). *The Handbook of Pragmatics*. Oxford: Blackwell, pp. 3–28.

Horn, Laurence R. 2006. The border wars: A neo-Gricean perspective. In: Klaus von Heusinger and Ken Turner (eds). *Where Semantics Meets Pragmatics: The Michigan Papers*. Oxford: Elsevier, pp. 21–48.

Hughes, Scarlett. 2008. 'RuPaul's Drag Race'! *Right TV*. https://web.archive.org/web/20120403120950/http://tv.rightcelebrity.com/rupauls-drag-race/201 [Accessed 25 January 2022].

Jacobs, Scott and Sally Jackson. 1983. Strategy and structure in conversational influence attempts. *Communication Monographs* 50(4): 285–304. https://doi .org/10.1080/03637758309390171.

Jaszczolt, Kasia M. 2005. *Default Semantics: Foundations of a Compositional Theory of Acts of Communication*. Oxford: Oxford University Press.

Jaszczolt, Kasia M. 2009. Cancelability and the primary/secondary meaning distinction. *Intercultural Pragmatics* 6(3): 259–89. https://doi.org/10.1515/ IPRG.2009.015.

Jaszczolt, Kasia M. 2010. Default Semantics. In: Bernd Heine and Heiko Narrog (eds). *The Oxford Handbook of Linguistic Analysis*. Oxford: Oxford University Press, pp. 193–221.

Jaszczolt, Kasia M. 2012. Context: Gricean intentions vs. two-dimensional semantics. In: Rita Finkbeiner, Jorg Meibauer and Petra B. Schumacher (eds). *What Is A Context? Linguistic Approaches and Challenges*. Amsterdam: John Benjamins, pp. 81–104.

Jaszczolt, Kasia M. 2023. *Semantics, Pragmatics, and Philosophy: A Journey Through Meaning*. Cambridge: Cambridge University Press.

Jaszczolt, Kasia M., Eleni Savva and Michael Haugh. 2016. The individual and the social path of interpretation: The case of incomplete disjunctive questions. In: Alessandro Capone and Jacob L. Mey (eds). *Interdisciplinary Studies in Pragmatics, Culture and Society*. Cham: Springer, pp. 251–83. https://doi.org/10.1007/978-3-319-12616-6_9.

Jefferson, Gail. 1987. On exposed and embedded correction in conversation. In: Graham Button and John R. E. Lee (eds). *Talk and Social Organisation*. Clevedon: Multilingual Matters, pp. 86–100.

Jefferson, Gail. 2003. A note on resolving ambiguity. In Phillip J. Glenn, Curtis D. LeBaron and Jenny Mandelbaum (eds.), *Studies in Language and Social Interaction*. Mahwah, NJ: Lawrence Erlbaum, pp. 221–40.

Jones, Taylor. 2016. Refining 'microaggression': A linguistic perspective. *Language Jones blog*. www.languagejones.com/blog-1/2016/9/8/ oi6379payz9mb4diadulndc244gq1s [Accessed 6 March 2022].

Kahneman, Daniel and Amos Tversky. 1979. Prospect theory: An analysis of decision under risk. *Econometrica* 47(2): 263–92. https://doi.org/10.2307/ 1914185.

Kulka, Rebecca. 2014. Performative force, convention, and discursive injustice. *Hypatia* 29(2): 440–57. https://doi.org/10.1111/j.1527-2001.2012.01316.x.

Lakoff, Robin. 1973. The logic of politeness; or, minding your p's and q's. *Papers from the 9th Regional Meeting*, Chicago Linguistic Society, pp. 292–305.

Langton, Rae. 1993. Speech acts and unspeakable acts. *Philosophy and Public Affairs* 22(4): 293–330.

Leech, Geoffrey. 1983. *Principles of Pragmatics*. London: Longman.

Lerner, Gene H. 2004. Collaborative turn sequences. In: Gene H. Lerner (ed). *Conversation Analysis: Studies from the First Generation*. Amsterdam: John Benjamins, pp. 225–56. https://doi.org/10.1075/pbns.125.12ler.

Levinson, Stephen C. 2000. *Presumptive Meanings: The Theory of Generalized Conversational Implicature*. Cambridge, MA: MIT Press.

Macagno, Fabrizio. 2023. Practical (un)cancellability. *Journal of Pragmatics* 215: 84–95. https://doi.org/10.1016/j.pragma.2023.07.010.

Mahon, James Edwin. 2016. The definition of lying and deception. In: Edward N. Zalta (ed). *The Stanford Encyclopedia of Philosophy* (Winter 2016 ed.). https://plato.stanford.edu/archives/win2016/entries/lying-definition/.

Mandelbaum, Jenny. 2016. Delicate matters: Embedded self-correction as a method for adjusting possibly available inapposite hearings. In Jeffrey D. Robinson (ed.). *Accountability in Social Interaction*. Oxford: Oxford University Press, pp. 108–137. https://doi.org/10.1093/acprof:oso/9780190210557.003.0004.

Mazzarella, Diana. 2021. 'I didn't mean to suggest anything like that!': Deniability and context reconstruction. *Mind & Language* 218–36. https://doi.org/10.1111/mila.12377.

Mazzarella, Diana, Robert Reinecke, Ira Noveck and Hugo Mercier. 2018. Saying, presupposing and implicating: How pragmatics modulates commitment. *Journal of Pragmatics* 133: 15–27. https://doi.org/10.1016/j.pragma.2018.05.009.

Mazzone, Marco. 2018. *Cognitive Pragmatics: Mindreading, Inferences, Consciousness*. Berlin: Walter de Gruyter.

McClure, Emma and Regina Rini. 2020. Microaggression: Conceptual and scientific issues. *Philosophy Compass* 15(4): e12659. https://doi.org/10.1111/phc3.12659.

Meibauer, Jörg. 2018. The Linguistics of Lying. *Annual Review of Linguistics* 4: 357–75. https://doi.org/10.1146/annurev-linguistics-011817-045634.

Miss AlexisMateo. 2021. The Queens Review (RuPauls Drag Race) season 13 Ruveal. *YouTube video*. https://youtu.be/Opdv7Qv9ZzM [Accessed 7 March 2022].

Moeschler, Jacques. 2013. Is a speaker-based pragmatics possible? Or how can a hearer infer a speaker's commitment? *Journal of Pragmatics* 48: 84–97. https://doi.org/10.1016/j.pragma.2012.11.019.

Morency, Patrick, Steve Oswald and Louis de Saussure. 2008. Explicitness, implicitness and commitment attribution: A cognitive pragmatic perspective.

Belgian Journal of Linguistics 22: 197–219. https://doi.org/10.1075/bjl.22.10mor.

Orr, Shirly, Mira Ariel and Orna Peleg. 2017. The case of literally true propositions with false implicatures. In: Innocent Chiluwa (ed). *Deception and Deceptive Communication: Motivations, Recognition Techniques and Behavioral Control*. New York: Nova Science, pp. 67–108.

Pinker, Steven. 2007. The evolutionary social psychology of off-record indirect speech acts. *Intercultural Pragmatics* 4(4): 437–61. https://doi.org/10.1515/IP.2007.023.

Pinker, Steven, Martin A. Nowak and James J. Lee. 2008. The logic of indirect speech. *Proceedings of the National Academy of Sciences* 105(3): 833–8. https://doi.org/10.1073/pnas.0707192105.

Recanati, François. 2002. Does linguistic communication rest on inference? *Mind & Language* 17(1–2): 105–26. https://doi.org/10.1111/1468-0017.00191.

Recanati, François. 2004. *Literal Meaning*. Cambridge: Cambridge University Press.

Recanati, François. 2010. *Truth-Conditional Pragmatics*. Oxford: Clarendon Press.

Reins, Louisa M. and Alex Wiegmann. 2021. Is lying bound to commitment? Empirically investigating deceptive presuppositions, implicatures, and actions. *Cognitive Science* 45(2): 1–35. https://doi.org/10.1111/cogs.12936.

RuPaul's Drag Race. 2020. Meet the queens of season 13! *YouTube video*. https://youtu.be/ZJRlvMURe_0 [Accessed 7 March 2022].

Sacks, Harvey, Emmanuel A. Schegloff and Gail Jefferson, 1974. A simplest systematics for the organization of turn-taking for conversation. *Language* 50(4): 696–735.

Sanders, Robert E. 1987. *Cognitive Foundations of Calculated Speech*. Albany: State University of New York Press.

Sanders, Robert E. 2013. The duality of speaker meaning: What makes self repair, insincerity, and sarcasm possible. *Journal of Pragmatics* 48(1): 112–22. https://doi.org/10.1016/j.pragma.2012.11.020.

Sanders, Robert E. 2015. A tale of two intentions: Intending what an utterance means and intending what an utterance achieves. *Pragmatics and Society* 6(4): 475–501. https://doi.org/10.1075/ps.6.4.01san.

Saul, Jennifer Mather. 2012. *Lying, Misleading, and What Is Said: An Exploration in Philosophy of Language and Ethics*. Oxford: Oxford University Press.

Savva, Eleni. 2017. *Subsentential Speech from a Contextualist Perspective*. PhD thesis, University of Cambridge.

Schegloff, Emanuel A. 1968. Sequencing in conversational openings. *American Anthropologist* 70: 1075-95.

Schegloff, Emanuel A. 1981. Discourse as an interactional achievement: Some uses of uh huh and other things that come between sentences. In: Deborah Tannen (ed). *Analyzing Discourse: Text and Talk*. Washington, DC: Georgetown University Press, pp. 71–93.

Schegloff, Emanuel. 1997. Third turn repair. In: Gregory R. Guy, Crawford Feagin, Deborah Schiffrin and John Baugh (eds). *Towards a Social Science of Language: Papers in Honour of William Labov. Volume 2: Social Interaction and Discourse Structures*. Amsterdam: John Benjamins, pp. 31–40.

Schegloff, Emanuel A. and Harvey Sacks. 1973. Opening up Closings. *Semiotica* 8: 289–327. http://dx.doi.org/10.1515/semi.1973.8.4.289.

Sperber, Dan and Deirdre Wilson. 1986/1995. *Relevance: Communication and Cognition*. Oxford: Basil Blackwell.

Sperber, Dan and Deirdre Wilson. 2002. Pragmatics, modularity and mind-reading. *Mind & Language* 17 (1–2): 3–23. https://doi.org/10.1111/1468-0017.00186

Sperber, Dan and Deirdre Wilson. 2015. Beyond speaker's meaning. *Croatian Journal of Philosophy* 15(44): 117–49. https://doi.org/10.5840/croatjphil20151528.

Stanley, Jason. 2000. Context and logical form. *Linguistics and Philosophy* 23: 391–434. https://doi.org/10.1023/A:1005599312747.

Stanley, Jason and Zoltán Gendler Szabó. 2000. On quantifier domain restriction. *Mind & Language* 15(2–3): 219–61. https://doi.org/10.1111/1468-0017.00130.

Sternau, Marit, Mira Ariel, Rachel Giora and Ofer Fein. 2015. Levels of interpretation: New tools for characterizing intended meanings. *Journal of Pragmatics* 84: 86–101. https://doi.org/10.1016/j.pragma.2015.05.002.

Sternau, Marit, Mira Ariel, Rachel Giora and Ofer Fein. 2017. Deniability and explicatures. In: Rachel Giora and Michael Haugh (eds). *Doing Intercultural Pragmatics: Cognitive, Linguistic, and Sociopragmatic Perspectives on Language Use*. Berlin: Mouton de Gruyter, pp. 97–120.

Stokke, Andreas. 2013. Lying, deceiving, and misleading. *Philosophy Compass* 8(4): 348–59. https://doi.org/10.1111/phc3.12022.

Stokke, Andreas. 2018. *Lying and Insincerity*. Oxford: Oxford University Press.

Sue, Derald Wing. 2010. *Microaggressions in Everyday Life: Race, Gender, and Sexual Orientation*. Hoboken, NJ: John Wiley.

Terkourafi, Marina. 2014. The importance of being indirect: A new nomenclature for indirect speech. *Belgian Journal of Linguistics* 28: 45–70. https://doi .org/10.1075/bjl.28.03ter.

Terkourafi, Marina. 2021. Inference and implicature. In Michael Haugh, Dániel Z. Kádár, Marina Terkourafi (eds). *The Cambridge Handbook of Sociopragmatics*. Cambridge: Cambridge University Press, pp. 30–47.

Townsend, Leanne and Claire Wallace. 2016. Social media research: A guide to ethics. www.gla.ac.uk/media/media_487729_en.pdf [Accessed 7 March 2022].

Viebahn, Emanuel. 2021. The lying-misleading distinction: A commitment-based approach. *The Journal of Philosophy* 118(6): 289–319. https://doi.org/ 10.5840/jphil2021118621.

Weissman, Benjamin and Marina Terkourafi. 2018. Are false implicatures lies? An empirical investigation. *Mind & Language* 34(2): 221–46. https://doi.org/ 10.1111/mila.12212.

Wiegmann, Alex, Pascale Willemsen and Jörg Meibauer. 2021. Lying, deceptive implicatures, and commitment. *Ergo* 8(50): 709–40. https://doi.org/ 10.3998/ergo.2251.

Williams, Bernard. 2002. *Truth and Truthfulness: An Essay in Genealogy*. Princeton: Princeton University Press.

Wilson, Deirdre. 2018. Relevance theory and literary interpretation. In: Terence Cave and Deirdre Wilson (eds). *Reading beyond the Code: Literature and Relevance Theory*. Oxford: Oxford University Press, pp. 185–204. https://doi.org/10.1093/oso/9780198794776.003.0011.

Wilson, Deirdre and Dan Sperber. 2002. Truthfulness and relevance. *Mind* 111(443): 583–632. https://doi.org/10.1093/mind/111.443.583.

Wilson, Deirdre and Dan Sperber. 2004. Relevance Theory. In: Laurence R. Horn and Gregory Ward (eds). *The Handbook of Pragmatics*. Oxford: Blackwell Publishing, pp. 607-632.

Wilson, Deirdre and Robyn Carston. 2006. Metaphor, relevance and the 'emergent property' issue. *Mind & Language* 21(3): 404–33. https://doi.org/ 10.1111/j.1468-0017.2006.00284.x.

Yuan, Wen and Siqi Lyu. 2022. Speech act matters: Commitment to what's said or what's implicated differs in the case of assertion and promise. *Journal of Pragmatics* 191: 128–42. https://doi.org/10.1016/j.pragma.2022.01.012.

Acknowledgements

I am grateful to the series editors, anonymous reviewers, as well as my colleagues Kasia Jaszczolt and Andreas Musolff for their detailed readings and feedback on previous versions of this manuscript. All remaining errors are, of course, my own.

Cambridge Elements

Pragmatics

Jonathan Culpeper

Lancaster University, UK

Jonathan Culpeper is Professor of English Language and Linguistics in the Department of Linguistics and English Language at Lancaster University, UK. A former co-editor-in-chief of the *Journal of Pragmatics* (2009–14), with research spanning multiple areas within pragmatics, his major publications include: *Impoliteness: Using Language to Cause Offence* (2011, CUP) and *Pragmatics and the English Language* (2014, Palgrave; with Michael Haugh).

Michael Haugh

University of Queensland, Australia

Michael Haugh is Professor of Linguistics and Applied Linguistics in the School of Languages and Cultures at the University of Queensland, Australia. A former co-editor-in-chief of the *Journal of Pragmatics* (2015–2020), with research spanning multiple areas within pragmatics, his major publications include: *Understanding Politeness* (2013, CUP; with Dániel Kádár), *Pragmatics and the English Language* (2014, Palgrave; with Jonathan Culpeper), and *Im/politeness Implicatures* (2015, Mouton de Gruyter).

Advisory Board

About the Series

The Cambridge Elements in Pragmatics series showcases dynamic and high-quality original, concise and accessible scholarly works. Written for a broad pragmatics readership it encourages dialogue across different perspectives on language use. It is a forum for cutting-edge work in pragmatics: consolidating theory (especially through cross-fertilization), leading the development of new methods, and advancing innovative topics in pragmatics.

Cambridge Elements ☰

Pragmatics

Elements in the Series

Printed in the United States
by Baker & Taylor Publisher Services